HISTORY OF THE WORLD

VOLUME II

3000 B.C. Sailors from Asia Minor land on Greece and settle there.

2200-1400 B.C. Crete at the height of power in the Aegean. Great palaces at Knossos and Phaestus built.

1500 B.C. Achaean kings build stronghold at Mycenae.

1400 B.C. Destruction of palaces at Knossos and Phaestus, probably by Greek raiders from the Peloponnesus. Decline of Cretan civilization.

1400-1200 B.C. Age of Mycenae.

1185 B.C. Troy destroyed by Achaeans.

1100 B.C. Dorian invasion of Achaean cities. Mycenae destroyed.

1000 B.C. Dark Ages of Greece. Dorians invade Peloponnesus, Crete, and Rhodes; Aeolians invade Thessaly and Boeotia; Ionians from Attica cross to Western shore of Asia Minor.

800-700 B.C. Formation of the city states and rise of aristocrats.

800-600 B.C. Colonization begins as Greece becomes overpopulated.

IN GREEK HISTORY, 3000 B.C.-485 B.C.

776 B.C. First Olympic games said to be held.

750 B.C. Homer writes *The Iliad* and *The Odyssey*.

621 B.C. Draco writes a code of harsh laws for Athens.

594 B.C. Solon is chosen to lead Athenians and replaces Draco's laws with a code of his own.

561 B.C. Pisistratus becomes tyrant of Athens.

544 B.C. After being exiled, Pisistratus returns and is tyrant again.

528 B.C. Death of Pisistratus.

507 B.C. Sparta invades Attica and brings about the fall of the tyrant sons of Pisistratus. Cleisthenes leads Athens towards democracy.

499 B.C. Athens and Eretria send help to Ionians resisting Darius of Persia.

492 B.C. First attack by Darius against Athens and Eretria.

490 B.C. Eretria is burned in Darius' second attack. The Athenians win the Battle of Marathon.

485 B.C. Darius dies and is succeeded by Xerxes.

HISTORY OF

Editor	Irwin Shapiro
Associate Editor	Jonathan Bartlett
Consultant	Albert Fried
	Department of History,
	Queens College, New York
Contributors	Anne Howard Bailey
	John Bowman
	Ormonde de Kay, Jr.
	Edith Firoozi
	Albert Fried
	Johanna Johnston
	Ira N. Klein
	Willis Lindquist
	Edna Ritchie
	Seymour Reit
	James L. Steffensen

VOLUME II

THE UNIVERSAL

THE WORLD

ANCIENT GREECE

by James L. Steffensen

Research Assistant,
PETER C. SACCIO

GOLDEN PRESS NEW YORK

CONTENTS

ANCIENT GREECE

MAP SHOWS THE MOUNTAINS AND THE SEAS WHICH GREATLY
INFLUENCED THE DEVELOPMENT OF ANCIENT GREECE.

The Silent Peninsula

3000 B.C.-1600 B.C.

ABOUT 3000 B.C., when the Pharaohs ruled
Egypt and Bablyon was the home of mighty
kings, bands of sailors set out from Asia Minor.

They followed a little chain of islands that led
northward across the unexplored sea that, centuries later, would be called the Mediterranean.
If the islands had not been there, the sailors
would never have dared to sail so far from
home. Asia, the only world they knew, stopped
at the eastern shore of the sea.

Some of the men were afraid that they might
suddenly reach the end of the world and drop

over it into nothing, but their captains ordered them to sail on. Their own countries were becoming crowded, and it was important to find new lands. So long as another island lay ahead of them, it seemed safe to go on. At last, their ships did indeed come to the end of the sea—but it was not the edge of the world. The sailors sighted a new mainland. It was the mountainous peninsula that would be given the name of Greece.

It was a strange and silent country of white stone peaks that disappeared into the clouds. Its thick forests of oaks and pines ran down to an oddly ragged coastline. The mountains, too, were jagged, as though an angry giant had smashed them.

GODS AND GIANTS

Years later, the people of Greece told a story about evil giants who fought a great battle with the gods to see which of them would rule the earth. The giants were defeated, and the gods locked them forever in a cave far under the ground. But the giants lived on, the storytellers said. When their anger took hold of them, they beat against the roof of their prison, and the earth shook. Land slid down the hillsides into the sea, and fire exploded from the mountaintops. The story was partly true, for Greece was a place of volcanoes and earthquakes. The peninsula's mountain ranges were twisted and broken. But the fields along the lower slopes of the mountains were rich, and the ragged coastline provided many fine, sheltered harbors.

Before long, people from Asia Minor began to settle in Greece. At first there were few of them, but they kept coming for nearly a thousand years. The new country seemed to welcome them. It gave them long months of sunshine to ripen their crops. The little valleys, like pockets between the mountains, were good, safe places for building towns. The settler planted olive trees on the slopes and set out grapevines in the fields. The forests rang with the sound of their bronze axes as they cut down trees to make frameworks for houses. Gradually the people forgot their old homes. They no longer thought of themselves as Asians. They were now called the Shore People, for they seldom went far from the shore or the southern part of the peninsula.

Inland and to the north, Greece was just as it had been when the sailors had discovered it. Only the wind in the green darkness of the forests and the sea slapping against the rocks broke the stillness. But beyond the silent mountains lay the vast continent of Europe, where things were far from quiet. Like a giant who had awakened from sleep, the great continent was restless and beginning to look around. But Europe was a wilderness, while Asia already had cities and powerful kingdoms. The Asians lived together in towns. They had learned how to plant and harvest crops on their sunny plains. They could read and write, and they understood arithmetic. They used money in their trading.

The Europeans knew none of these things. They were barbaric warriors, who lived with the cunning and ferocity of the wild beasts they hunted with their spears. Europe had harsh winters and nature was an enemy. Food was scarce. A man, like an animal, had to be a fighter to live. He and the other men of his family—his sons and brothers and cousins—banded together in packs like wolves. They roamed the hills and swept down on other family tribes, killing them for a hunting ground or a place which gave some shelter against the cold. Their clothes were the skins of animals. Their houses, when they had them, were huts made of sticks and mud. But usually they were on the move, searching for food, fighting the tribes they met along the trail, always wandering. Some of them turned south toward Spain and Italy and Greece, the three fingers of Europe which reached into the Mediterranean. Steep mountains guarded the northern ends of the peninsulas, discouraging the wanderers from going farther. But, in time, the tribesmen discovered passes through the mountains. With their bronze swords, they fought their way down the peninsulas. In Spain and Italy they built huts and lived as they had always done. But in Greece, they came upon the Shore People. For the first time, the men of the East and the men of the West met face to face, and the Europeans learned about the Asian world of cities.

A NEW NATION

More tribesmen came through the mountains from Europe. They were savage fighters who had horses, which the Asians had never seen before.

They took the northern mainland of Greece, then moved south to the Peloponnesus. The Peloponnesus was a large mass of land which the earthquakes had almost separated from the rest of Greece. Only the Isthmus, a narrow strip of land, connected it to the mainland. Except for the Isthmus, it would have been an island. The tribesmen claimed the Peloponnesus as their own, but they did not kill off the Shore People. Instead, they kept them to be their farmers and craftsmen, taught them their language, and gradually took them into their family tribes. A new nation of men was born—the Greeks.

The world was never the same after that. When the two kinds of people, whose ways were so different, came together, something happened. It was like a flint struck against granite to make fire. But the fire of the Greeks burned with ideas—ideas in philosophy and science and art. In centuries to come they wrote plays and poetry, and designed the most beautiful buildings the world had seen. They thought about freedom and de-

THE GREEKS BELIEVED THE GODS ONCE FOUGHT GIANTS FOR THE RULE OF THE WORLD.

mocracy, and acted on these thoughts. From one little peninsula, the fire of the Greeks spread to all of Europe, and then to the Americas.

But the beginning was slow, and the Greeks' first years were hard. They were years of learning to live in a new land and to grow strange crops; years of learning to build cities and to live together peacefully; years of fighting off new invaders or moving on if the invaders were too strong. Most of all, they were years in which the Greeks learned about the sea.

When the tribesmen first came from Europe, they knew nothing about sailing. Greece soon turned them into seamen, for the sea was the highway of the ancient world. It led the Greeks to the crops and markets of other lands, to the gold and wisdom of the cities of the East. And it led them to war, for they were newcomers to the seas, and they had to fight the people who had already set up trade routes. The strongest of these people, the men whom the Greeks met first in trade and battle, were the sea-warriors of Crete.

THE BATTLE WAS DEPICTED IN THIS FRIEZE FROM A TEMPLE IN SACRED DELPHI.

The Power
of Minos

2200 B.C.-1400 B.C.

FAR TO the south of the Greek peninsula lay the large island of Crete. It was the home of a nation of sea-warriors—cruel, dark, handsome men, who claimed the eastern Mediterranean and all of the Aegean Sea as their own. For eight hundred years—from 2200 to 1400 B.C.—they made that claim good.

The Cretan seamen strutted about the decks in loincloths and high boots. They wore clanking jewelry of finely worked gold, curled their long hair, and rubbed their bodies with perfumed oil so that they glistened in the sunlight. But they were fighters, and they knew every trick of sailing and of piracy. With the sharp bronze prows of their warships, they smashed the sides of the ships which dared to meet them in battle.

No one could remember when they had first come to Crete. Perhaps they had once been Asians, but the island had been their home as far back as 4000 B.C. At first, they had been farmers. Then they had discovered the gold that waited at the ends of the sea lanes. They began to sell pottery and olive oil to the rich Egyptians. As they grew more daring, they went trading along the coasts of the Aegean Sea. By 1700 B.C., their sleek merchant ships were the best vessels afloat, and their battleships were the strongest. By 1600 B.C., when the Greeks were cautiously trying out clumsy little boats that wobbled in the waves, the king of Crete could call the whole Aegean Sea his private empire.

As soon as the little towns in Greece seemed wealthy enough to make good customers, the Cretan merchants came calling with things to sell—delicate pottery, brightly painted with flowers and sea creatures; leather armor with bronze plates for extra protection; and jewelry of gold, silver, and a rare, precious metal called tin. The Greeks were delighted with the Cretan goods and bought all they could afford. When the next trading ship appeared on the horizon, the townspeople rushed to the shore, eager to buy and to hear the news of the world beyond their shores.

But the Cretans who first came as merchants often came back as bullies and robbers. They treated the Greeks scornfully and threatened them until they were given gold. Sometimes they kidnapped children and took them to Crete to serve as slaves. The little towns were too weak to do anything about it, and a Cretan sail on the horizon became a signal of danger. The townsmen hid their families and waited in fear as the ship came in to land.

The Greeks never forgot the stories of the horrors of Crete. Long after the Cretans had lost

THE CRETANS PAID THEIR TAXES WITH OLIVE OIL, GRAIN, AND WINE, WHICH THEY BROUGHT TO THE KING'S PALACE IN KNOSSOS. IN THE FOREGROUND, A CRETAN PRINCE OF THE 15TH CENTURY B.C.

A CRETAN PAINTING OF THE 15TH CENTURY B.C.
SHOWS THE DANGEROUS SPORT OF BULL-DANCING.

their power, people on the mainland still talked about the Minotaur, the monster that the king of Crete kept in his great city, Knossos. The Minotaur, they said, had the body of a man and the head of a bull. He lived on human flesh. Each year a black ship of war was sent from Knossos to Greece to collect the sacrifices for the monster. At every town, the captain demanded to see the children. He chose the seven handsomest youths and the seven prettiest girls, and sailed away with them. At Knossos, the children were sent into the Labyrinth, a building with so many rooms and hallways that no one who went into it ever found his way out again. There the Minotaur waited, and when his lost and frightened victims came upon him, he killed them.

THE REAL MINOTAUR

It was only a legend, of course. But Greek legends were full of history, and the tales that seem the most fantastic often came the closest to the truth. The Minotaur was an imaginary beast, but the Cretan priests who wore masks in the shape of a bull's head were real. The monster's name meant "the bull of Minos," and Minos was the name of a king of Crete, a ruler who was so famous that the Greeks began to call his people "Minoans." This king did have a kind of labyrinth—his enormous palace at Knossos. From his

throne room, hundreds of rooms and hallways and courtyards spread across five acres of land.

To a Greek, who knew only the rough fortresses of the mainland, such a place must indeed have seemed a labyrinth in which he could get lost and never find his way out. As he wandered through it, he would have come upon religious shrines decorated with the great double-edged axes which were the sacred sign of Crete. They were called *labrys*. On the palace walls, he would have seen paintings of athletes leaping around huge bulls and grasping their horns to somersault over their backs. There, perhaps, was the truth behind the story of the young Greeks who were taken away in the black ship. In Knossos, they were trained to become "bull-dancers" for the entertainment of the Minoan king and his noblemen. When they were sent into the arena with one of the ferocious black bulls, they teased him until he rushed at them; then they jumped away from his sharp horns or caught at the horns and flipped themselves over his head. It was a dangerous sport, and sooner or later the dancers were killed. For the stranger from Greece, wandering through the palace, the paintings of the bull-dancers were a bitter reminder of the cruelty of King Minos and of his power over the Greeks.

A lone stranger could not wander far, however, nor did he have much chance to get lost. The palace was bustling with people to show him the way, and there were guards at many of the doors.

The Power of Minos

The palace was the center of a rich, busy city. From the cool veranda next to his royal chambers, King Minos looked down on rows of handsome houses. Many were two or three stories tall, with wide windows and tree-shaded terraces. No wall circled the town or the palace. Minos said that his ships were his wall; they were strong enough to frighten away or destroy any invader.

Life was comfortable in Knossos. When a man was home from a voyage, he could enjoy himself. There were feasts and processions. Dressed in glittering costumes, the people marched singing through the great, bright halls of the palace. Royal banquets were noisy affairs, with plenty of food and strong wine, followed by dancing. The gold necklaces and bracelets of the dancers caught the flickering light of the torches and jangled in time to the music.

The palace had a theater, and an arena for games like the bull-dancing. But bull-dancing was more than a sport. Sometimes a bull was killed, and his blood offered as a sacrifice to the Lady of

AT THE ANNUAL HARVEST FESTIVAL, THE FIRST FRUITS WERE PRESENTED TO KING MINOS.

the Wild Creatures, the mother of the earth, who was the most important Minoan goddess.

There was a Minoan god, too—a young man. He may have stood for the king, a god on earth, but he was not as powerful as the great goddess. Minoan women did not let their husbands forget that. They reminded the men that, in some places where the goddess was worshiped, women ran things and their husbands did as they were told. That was not true in Crete. There, men and women were equals—but the ladies insisted on their rights. They dressed themselves in fashionable long, flounced skirts and tight bodices, put up their hair, and joined in the feasting at the palace just as the men did.

For 300 years or more, there were good times at Knossos. The king ruled the Aegean, and his ships came home laden with the riches of the world. Then it all changed.

THE FALL OF KNOSSOS

There was another chapter in the legend of Crete, a final chapter. The storytellers said that Theseus, a young Greek prince, was brought to Knossos as a sacrifice to the Minotaur. Like so many prisoners before him, he was put into the Labyrinth. But Theseus was a favorite of the gods. When he came upon the Minotaur, he did not cower or try to flee. Instead, he fought the monster with his bare hands and killed him. With the death of the Minotaur, King Minos' power was broken. His palace was destroyed, his warships

INVADERS BURNED AND SACKED THE PALACE AT KNOSSOS ABOUT 1400 B.C.

were defeated in battle, and Theseus, a Greek, became the ruler of Crete.

No one knows how it actually happened, but the power of Crete and its navy was broken. Knossos fell about 1400 B.C. The palace without a wall was invaded and burned, probably by Greek raiders from the Peloponnesus. The Greeks had learned to build good ships and were no longer afraid to fight. Minoan ships disappeared from the sea, and the Minoans themselves began to be forgotten. Crete became just another Greek island.

Companions of the King

1500 B.C. - 1000 B.C.

GOLD MASK FOUND IN A GRAVE AT MYCENAE

ACROSS the plains of the Peloponnesus flashed the swift chariots of knights and warrior-princes. They wore armor of gleaming bronze, and bright, proud plumes bobbed above their helmets. They were the new men of a new country, and they called themselves the Achaeans. Their kings called themselves the Sons of Pelops, the mighty chief and hero who had given his name to the Peloponnesus.

Pelops, the Achaeans said, was the son of a god. Probably, however, he was the grandson of a European invader, for many of the Achaeans' ancestors were barbarian invaders from the north. But they may have seemed like gods to the Shore People when they first hacked their way into the country. Their ragged beards and horned helmets were frightening to look at, and they fought like demons. They took the land they wanted, built fortresses, and settled down to stay. When Minoan sailor-merchants began to stop at their towns, the warriors went into business, growing olives and squeezing them in presses to make oil. Olive oil was the butter, cooking grease, lamp fuel, and hair tonic of the ancient world, and the Achaeans began to grow rich.

For a hundred years, from 1500 to 1400 B.C., Achaean kings built a stronghold at Mycenae, not far from the Isthmus, the strip of land that connected the Peloponnesus to the mainland. The new castle, towering above the plain, had room inside to shelter all the people of Mycenae. Its huge walls looked like cliffs, and people said that the stones had been put there by the Cyclops, the one-eyed giants whose parents were the gods of the earth and sky. When the king's trumpets sounded the warning that an enemy was near, farmers ran from their fields, and potters and armorers left their shops at the base of the castle hill. They crowded through the castle gates. Some clutched their children and their most precious possessions in their arms. Others tugged at their animals, for there was space inside the walls for the cattle as well as the people. Food enough for everyone had already been stored on the castle hill, along with the city's valuable supply of olive oil. A well had been chipped through hundreds of feet of rock to provide a safe supply of water. Once the gates were pushed shut, with millstones and boulders heaped up against them, the king and his people could wait out an enemy siege for weeks or months. They could fight back, too. Soldiers who tried to storm the gates were easy targets for the archers stationed on the high walls. Anyone who tried to climb the wall itself met a

103

(RIGHT) RUINS OF THE FAMOUS LION'S GATE OF THE PALACE AT MYCENAE. (BELOW) STATUE OF WARRIORS IN A CHARIOT DRAWN BY FOUR HORSES

deadly rain of rocks and flaming logs or oil. If someone managed to climb up to the top, the defenders were ready with axes to split his helmet and his head.

The defenses of the castle were so strong, in fact, that they were seldom used. Enemies stayed away, and the strangers who came to Mycenae came in peace. They were given a very different sort of greeting. Every man, when he had spoken his name and sworn that he had come as a friend, was treated courteously. An important visitor—anyone who came in a chariot—was welcomed with ceremony and allowed to drive up the ramp into the courtyard of the palace. He entered by the main gate, where two lions carved from a huge slab of limestone stood guard above the gateway. From the Lions' Gate he was led across the courtyard, through other strong gateways, to the great front door of the palace.

This building was as splendid as any that King Minos could have imagined. Slabs of gleaming white limestone hid the rocks and wooden posts which gave strength to its walls. The floors, ceilings, and walls inside were covered with paintings and colored stucco. In the first of the royal chambers, where a guest waited until he was summoned to the throne room, there were soft couches for visitors. The Achaeans still kept the custom of sleeping in the great hall or *megaron;* this outer chamber was the palace "guest room." If the visitor was tired and dusty from his journey, he was offered a bath before he went to meet the king. And if he was an important person, he took his bath in the royal bathroom, a large, bright room with an enormous clay tub standing in its center. Jars of steaming water stood at hand and there were servants to wait on him. There were oils to be added to the bath, and perfumes to sweeten it. When the guest was in the tub, he was offered a cup of wine to help him relax. After his bath, he was rubbed with more perfumed oils.

The Achaeans made the perfumed oil by adding herbs to plain olive oil. The herbs were gathered from the hills, where they grew in abundance. All the peoples of the Mediterranean loved perfumed oil. The Egyptians even made it into a thick cream, which was heaped on the heads of honored guests at feasts. As the evening went on, the cream would melt and run down their bodies.

And so the Achaeans became the oil traders of the world. They sold oil plain in big clay jars or perfumed in delicate, painted vases, and it made them rich. Mycenae's king was a merchant as well as a general and a chief. The deep cellars of his castle were filled with row upon row of oil jars. Dozens of clerks kept records of his collections, shipments, and sales. In the little accounting rooms near the palace entrance, they scratched the daily records on tablets of soft clay with pointed sticks. They also kept lists of the number of his chariots, the movement of his troops, the weapons sent to soldiers in the field, the furniture built for the palace, and the supply of golden wine cups. The lists were long, for Mycenae was the richest, strongest kingdom in Greece. Oil had paid for it all—the castle walls, the palace, and the splendid throne room to which the visitor was led, fresh from his bath.

The throne room remained a *megaron,* but it was bright with color and sparkling with jeweled decorations. Delicate patterns of sea animals and grasses wound across the floor and hearth at its center. The walls were covered with pictures of sacred and magical beasts. The throne itself was a huge wooden chair inlaid with battle scenes worked in gold, silver, and tin.

The men who stood about the throne were as different from the old barbaric warriors as their *megaron* was from the hall in the old fortress. The Achaeans had learned more than trading and seamanship from the Minoans. They had shaved off their beards and curled their hair. Like the Minoans, they now wore jeweled belts and short leather breeches.

In spite of their elegant dress, they were still warriors—a company of knights who gathered around the hearth in the *megaron.* They now fought with spears as well as swords, and they used small metal shields that allowed them to move quickly on the field. They also had bronze armor—breastplates decorated with gold and plumed helmets with long nosepieces and face protectors that wrapped around their jaws. Such armor was expensive and only the noblemen could afford to buy it. The noblemen were called the "Companions of the King," and it was their duty to protect the rest of his subjects. For battles were not fought by thousands of troops, but by a few noble knights who rode to war in chariots and challenged the knights of the enemy. Sometimes

kingdoms were gambled on the single combat of two men, each the champion of his own people.

In their palace halls, the knights still welcomed the minstrels, the wandering poets who played on small harps and chanted their verses in return for a meal and a place to sleep. And the minstrels, in turn, began to make up new poems about the Achaean champions. Of course, they still recited the stories of the gods and the ancient warriors. But now, as they journeyed from castle to castle, they added the adventures of the new heroes to their poems. Other poets heard them and wrote their own verses about the knights. The stories of the Achaeans, told and told again, became the legends of Greece—tales chanted in the glow of countless hearthfires.

THE TROJAN WAR

The favorite story, the one that every minstrel was sure to know, was about the Trojan War. It was a story of Achaean heroes who sailed across the Aegean Sea to attack a powerful fortress city, Troy, the home of a band of warriors as courageous and noble as the Achaeans themselves. There were many ways to tell the tale, but it always began, as had the war itself, with the king of Mycenae. He was a king who commanded kings, the man to whom other rulers turned for counsel and protection. His own city was so strong that years later, whenever the Greeks spoke of the time when the Achaeans ruled Greece, they called it the Mycenean Age. This great king's name was Agamemnon, and it was he who planned the attack on Troy. He called for all the Achaean fighting men to sail with him, and they came eagerly. They gathered at the seacoast, an army of the finest knights in the Peloponnesus. As they boarded the warships, the priests made their sacrifices. They prayed first—to the old Minoan goddess, the mother of the world and then called for the help of a new Greek god, Poseidon, the earthshaker and god of the sea. The ships began to move and the course was set for Troy.

When the fleet had crossed the Aegean, the Achaeans beached their boats, and moved across the plain toward Troy. But there they stopped, for the city walls were so tall and thick and strong that it was said they had been built by the gods. The Achaeans made their camp on the plain outside and besieged the city. But weeks passed, then months and years. The walls stood as strong as ever, with the Trojans locked in and Achaeans locked out. Knights on the plain shouted out their challenge, and Trojan guards hurled down their answers from the battlements. But an Achaean won one fight, a Trojan won the next, and nothing was settled.

So it went for ten years—from about 1194 to 1184 B.C. Then, suddenly, things changed. The minstrels said it was because the gods had decided in favor of the Achaeans. At last, Agamemnon's soldiers found a way into the city. Years later, when the story was told, no one could say exactly how it had been done. Some minstrels told of spies, who slipped past the Trojan guards and opened the gates at night. Others said that the Achaeans had found a weak place in the wall and crashed through. Still others told of a huge wooden horse which the Achaeans built. The soldiers left it standing on the plain, marched off to their boats, and set sail as though they were leaving Troy. But they left behind a small group of men, hidden in the hollow body of the horse. To the Trojans, who were certain that the Achaeans had given up the fight, the wooden horse seemed a token of peace or perhaps an offering to the gods. They hauled it into the city

THE CITY OF TROY RULED THE CHANNEL KNOWN AS THE HELLESPONT.

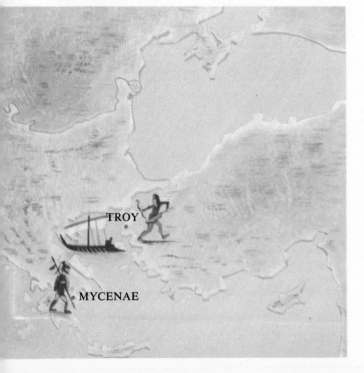

TROY

MYCENAE

as a victory prize. Late at night, when the guards were asleep or busy celebrating, the Achaeans hiding in the horse crept out through a trap door and hurried to open the gates of the city. The Achaean army had returned in the darkness and was waiting just outside.

Agamemnon's soldiers poured into Troy. They ran through the narrow streets, slashing at the Trojans with their battle-axes. They dragged the Trojan king and his archers off the wall, then tore down the wall itself and set fire to the houses. The Trojans were killed or ran away. When the city was in ruins, the victorious Achaeans gave thanks to the gods for their triumph, and then sailed for home.

So went the story, and much of it seems to have been true. There was actually a great fortress-city called Troy, and its people were well prepared for battle. They had to be prepared, for their city stood on the eastern bank of the Helles-pont, the narrow channel that led from the Aegean to the Black Sea. Beyond the channel lay the lands of strange tribes whose towns were rich and whose people were eager for trade. But the king who ruled Troy also ruled the channel. He alone decided which ships would sail through it and which had to turn back. Merchants wishing to trade in the Black Sea had to come to terms with the Trojan king first, and usually it was expensive. Many kings envied Troy's power over the Hellespont. Others simply wanted free passage through the channel. Some of them, like the Achaean kings, were willing to fight for it.

The ancestors of the Trojans had themselves come to Troy as invaders. They had built their stronghold on the ruins of the one they had destroyed, and below that lay the ruins of four even earlier Troys. When an earthquake knocked down the new city, the Trojans had had to build again—the seventh city on the pile. Its palace was tall and handsome, but its streets were narrow and the houses were small, roughly made, and crowded together. All of the architects' skill and the efforts of the workmen had gone into building the walls. They were as huge as the storytellers said they were—fifteen feet thick, twenty feet high, and topped with towers and platforms for archers. As for houses, it was enough that they were safely inside the walls and that the storage tanks under their floors were filled with food.

With such preparations, Troy could hold off an enemy siege for weeks or months. If the

ACCORDING TO LEGEND, THE WALLS OF TROY KEPT OUT THE ACHAEANS FOR TEN YEARS.

Achaeans did not actually camp outside the walls for ten years, they must surely have been forced to wait for a discouragingly long time. But they did find a way into the city at last, probably by breaking through the one weak spot in the wall. The section above the steepest face of the hill was slightly thinner than the rest, because no one thought that an enemy would attempt to attack from that side. The Achaeans had little time to enjoy their victory, however, for suddenly their own cities were in danger. A new mob of invaders had found the paths that led south through the mountains from Europe. They had come from the Danube country, the no man's land northeast of the mountains, and already they were fighting and plundering their way toward the Peloponnesus. Refugees, fleeing to the south, told terrible stories of the strength and cruelty of the invaders, whom they called the Dorians. They said that the Dorians were as fierce as the Achaeans' own barbaric ancestors. They said that they fought with swords made of a new metal, iron, that splintered the strongest bronze weapons.

The Achaeans prepared to defend themselves. Women and children from the country towns were brought to castle cities where they would be safe. Their husbands and brothers were sent to guard the seacoast and the Isthmus, the strip of land at the top of the Peloponnesus. The metalsmiths worked day and night, hammering out swords, axe heads, and shields. The kings' clerks scratched onto the clay tablets the records of chariots sent north, children moved south, arms heaped in the palace halls, and the oil that was to pay for it all.

Then the attack came. The Dorians swept across the Peloponnesus and nothing could stop them. When they surrounded the castles, the Achaeans inside lit bonfires, the signal that would bring troops from other strongholds. The only reply was the smoke of other bonfires, more cries for help. Later, there were still greater clouds of smoke and fires that lit the plains at night. Each meant a castle captured, its people murdered, and its buildings destroyed.

Mycenae was gone. Less than forty years after the time of Agamemnon, his kingdom was torn apart and his palace was a ruin. The great jars of oil made a white-hot fire when the Dorians tossed their torches into them. Timbers in the walls burst into flame, and the palace collapsed. Only the *tholos,* the great burial chambers built into the side of the castle hill, were safe, and the strange graves which the first kings had cut like wells into the rock beneath the palace. Hidden under the broken stones, they held the bodies of kings and treasures of gold, bronze, and painted pottery. In the ruins above, the clerks' little clay tablets were baked hard by the fire. In three thousand years, these things would be the proof that the legends of Agamemnon and the Achaeans were true.

The Dorians took almost all of the Peloponnesus. The Achaeans who survived were pushed into a little corner on the northwest coast. This was a time of wandering and killing, a Dark Age which began about 1000 B.C. and lasted nearly two hundred years.

As the Dorian warriors invaded other parts of the peninsula, the refugees moved on in search of

land. When there was no more room for them on the mainland, they set out across the Aegean Sea. From the burned-out highland cities, the tribes which called themselves the Aeolians went to Asia Minor. Other tribes, called the Ionians, were forced off their lands in Argolis and Attica, just northeast of the Isthmus. They, too, went to Asia Minor. Then the Dorians, not satisfied with owning the Peloponnesus, also took the two big islands of Crete and Rhodes. But gradually the invasions died down. The homeless found new homes. Settled in their new lands, the Aeolians, Ionians, and Dorians began to build. Little towns appeared, and then cities. The Dark Age was coming to an end, and the greatest age of Greece was beginning. The people of the new cities, though they belonged to rival tribes, all called themselves Greeks. They considered their cities part of the Greek world. It was a world that had spread until it now included all the lands surrounding the Aegean Sea, as well as including all the islands in it.

THE DARK AGE OF GREECE BEGAN WITH THE DORIAN INVASION.

108

Gods and Heroes

800 B.C.-550 B.C.

HYPNOS, THE GREEK GOD OF SLEEP

FROM island to island and town to town, across the wide new world of the Greeks, the minstrel wandered, with a harp slung across his back and a batch of stories in his hand. When he knocked at the gate of a palace or great house and offered to sing for his supper, he was never refused. There were no shows to see and no books to read. The people relied on the minstrels to entertain them and to tell the stories of the past, which otherwise might be forgotten.

The minstrel's stock of stories was a mixture of tall tales, half-remembered history, and myths, the stories of the gods. He collected them wherever he traveled, usually from other minstrels. As the stories were passed along from singer to singer, the history grew a little fuzzier and the tales grew a great deal taller.

In the great hall of a palace, where the lord and his guests gathered in the evening, the minstrel was given a place of honor. After dinner, he was invited to sing. Most of his songs began with the Achaean attack on Troy. First, he reminded his listeners of the reason for the war: Paris, a prince of Troy, stole Helen, the wife of the king of Sparta, Menelaus, and the most beautiful woman in the world. The minstrel told about Agamemnon's call to arms and the fleet that was made ready to sail. Then he listed the famous heroes who boarded the ships. Each had his own adventures, and the minstrel chose different ones to tell about every evening. He might sing about Agamemnon, who came home from Troy victorious, only to be killed by his wife; or Achilles, the greatest of Greek warriors, who slew the Trojan champion Hector; or Odysseus, the craftiest of the Greeks, whose journey home from Troy was a ten-year series of adventures. The minstrel put the stories together until he had a song long enough to fill an evening. The Greeks called him a *rhapsode*, a "stitcher together."

The most famous of the *rhapsodes* was Homer, an Ionian Greek from Asia Minor. No one knows which town he came from or exactly when he lived. About 750 B.C., he wrote down two of his stitched-together stories, and they became the story book, history, and bible of the Greek world. In a few years, everyone had heard of Homer's poems. Many people could recite them by heart, though they were thousands of lines long. All of the wonder and pride which the Greeks felt for their land and its heroes seemed to be in Homer's words.

THE *ILIAD* AND THE *ODYSSEY*

The stories were old ones that everybody knew. In the *Iliad*, Homer told about Achilles and his quarrel with Agamemnon over the booty they had taken from a town near Troy. Angry and insulted, Achilles refused to fight against the Trojans. The Greeks began to lose battles and many knights were killed, but Achilles would not change his mind. Not until his best friend was killed by Hector, the leader of the Trojan arms, did Achilles stir from his tent. Then his rage got the better of his pride and he went to the field to take out his anger on the Trojans and particularly on Hector.

To a child, the *Iliad* was just an exciting story. But when he went to school, he found it was his textbook. It taught him history, geography, and the honorable behavior expected of a Greek. As he grew older, he found new lessons in Homer's book. There was always a line somewhere to settle a dispute or advise him when he had a problem.

GREEK COLONISTS BROUGHT THEIR WAY OF LIFE TO SETTLEMENTS IN DISTANT LANDS.

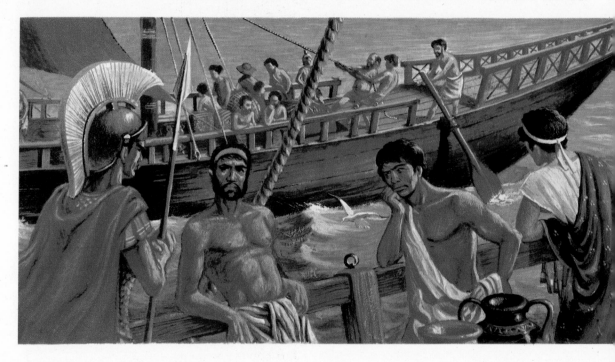

Homer's other book was a tale of adventures and a geography of the ancient world. The *Odyssey* told about Odysseus' ten years of roaming after the war. Cursed by the sea god Poseidon, he was driven far off course by storms, shipwrecked, and tossed onto the shores of mysterious islands. On one, he was chased by cannibals. On another he had to fight the Cyclops, the one-eyed giants. Witches disguised as beautiful girls tried to enchant him, and Poseidon did his best to kill him. But Athena, the goddess of wisdom, came to his aid and at last he returned to rule his kingdom in Greece.

THE WAYS OF THE GODS

Again, it was a good story. But it also helped to explain the ways of the gods, which were always a little puzzling. And the gods themselves were the explanation of an even greater puzzle. For, to the early Greeks, the world was a frightening place, and nature was full of mysteries they could not understand. The sea rose up and smashed their ships. The sun had been known to disappear from the sky at midday. Men were sometimes caught by feelings they could not control—by anger, by jealousy, by love.

The people could not believe that such things happened by accident. They must be the work of creatures more powerful than men—the gods. For example, the sea which sometimes rose in anger was the god Poseidon. The sun was the god Apollo, whose beams were golden arrows.

As they found gods to explain more of the mysteries of nature, the Greeks began to talk about a kingdom of gods. They said that Zeus, the king, was the sky god. He lived in a palace of clouds at the top of Mount Olympus. All of the other gods were his subjects, each with his own special duties. Hades guarded the underworld, the land of the dead. Zeus' queen, Hera, looked after babies and mothers. Demeter helped the crops grow, and Dionysus kept an eye on grapevines and wine. When people fell in love, they were under the spell of Aphrodite, the beautiful but fickle goddess of love. Her rival was Artemis, Apollo's twin sister. Although Artemis was the goddess of the moon, she was a clear-headed huntress who had no time for such nonsense as love.

Apollo himself was a special god for the people

who lived on earth. Farmers prayed to him to guard their fields. Shepherds asked his protection for their flocks. Lawmakers called him the god of discipline, who brought the light of order to a dark, wild world. Apollo could also foretell the future. When any man—even a king—had an important decision to make, he went to Apollo's temple at Delphi. There the Oracle, a mysterious priestess, spoke with the voice of the gods. In a cave beneath her shrine, the Oracle made her sacrifices and asked the questions which men wanted answered. Then she fell into a trance, shrieking strange messages which only the priests could understand. They explained the meaning to the men who had come for Apollo's help. Cities went to war or called their armies home, kings chose their heirs, and farmers chose a day on which to plant their crops according to the Oracle's advice. No man dared to disagree with what she said.

But it was difficult to deal with gods. They seemed to get angry for no reason and deserted their followers just when the need for help was greatest. The stories in Homer's poems helped to explain these things. The gods in his tales acted very much like human beings. Of course,

they were more beautiful and powerful than men, and they did not suffer pain or grow old and die. But Homer showed that they could feel and act like men. They bickered and quarreled, turned jealous, and picked sides in human quarrels or wars.

The gods were not examples of good behavior. Zeus, for instance, had fought his own father in order to make himself the king of the gods. As people read Homer, they learned that they must try to get along with the gods, not imitate them. They must respect the gods' power and try to please them, but they could not expect to be loved by them.

THE POWER OF POSEIDON

For men who explored the seas, Homer's tale of Odysseus had a special meaning. Like Odysseus, they went roaming the oceans beyond their familiar Aegean, guided by the stars and their own courage. Often tossed about by storms or blown far off course, they knew well the power of Poseidon, the god who controlled the waves. They had seen the Black Sea boil like a cauldron,

111

and along its shores they had found people as strange as any Odysseus had met.

Homer knew his geography. It was said that he himself had traveled some of the routes he described in his stories. He must also have listened carefully to the reports of adventurers who had been to the distant, unknown corners of the Mediterranean and Black seas. Many of the odd islands Homer wrote about turned up when the people of the new Greek cities sent their own scouts exploring far-off regions.

THE GREEK COLONISTS

Where the explorers went, colonists followed, to the Black Sea coasts and the western half of the Mediterranean. Most of the colonists were ordinary Greeks in search of new homes. Some left their cities because the laws did not suit them. Others went to find land. Some great cities

THIS HEAD OF THE POET HOMER DATES FROM THE 5TH CENTURY B.C.

planted colonies in places where they hoped to trade. The people of Miletus founded a chain of colonies along the Black Sea. The people of Megara, following the advice of the Oracle, built a town on the northern side of the channel between the Black Sea and the Aegean. The advice was good. The town, Byzantium, became an important city, and it remained important for more than 2,000 years.

Sicily and the southern tip of Italy, with their clear air and warm weather, were inviting places to the colonists. The Messenians from southern Greece built Messina on Sicily. Then the Corinthians built Syracuse, which became the largest city in the Greek world. Tarentum, Cumae, Tegium, and Neapolis sprang up in Italy. Eventually there were so many Greek cities in the region that it was called *Magna Graecia*, or "Greater Greece."

The colonizing began at the end of the Dark Age, about 800 B.C. It went on for nearly 250 years. Parents and children, farmers and craftsmen and statesmen braved the half-known oceans to find homes in strange new lands. They carried with them a cauldron of fire, lit from the sacred flame of the city they had left behind. At the end of the journey, it was used to start the fire on the altar-hearth of the new city. It did not matter that the settlers were far from their old homes. They had brought the arts and ways of Greece with them, along with their cooking pots and carpenters' tools. And if they ran into problems, there was always an answer in Homer.

Kings, Tyrants, and Democracy

1000 B.C. - 100 B.C.

DURING the Dark Age, the large kingdoms of Homer's Achaean heroes had disappeared. The Greek world was now dotted with dozens of little countries. They had begun with fortresses set on hills and crags. Soon each fortress was

GREEK POTTERS AT WORK IN THEIR SHOP

surrounded by a village, as farmers abandoned their huts in the fields and built new homes close to the walls. In times of danger, they could take refuge behind the walls. A market place was built, and a few metalsmiths and potters opened shops. When temples were set up inside the fortress, the castle hill became an acropolis, a "high-town," the sacred center of a kingdom as well as a place to hide from attackers. The village chief began to call himself a king.

THE NEW NOBLEMEN

In a kingdom not much bigger than a town, everyone could keep an eye on the king and his friends, the noblemen. The people watched their rulers carefully, for life in Greece was changing, and not always for the better. Food was scarce, and there was meat only on holidays. The rest of the year, the people ate mostly barley porridge, and sometimes fruit and olives. Even wheat was expensive, and no one had much money. The little kingdoms did not have enough olive trees to make them rich. Besides, the groves belonged to the noblemen, who never shared their profits.

These new noblemen were not knights. They managed the kingdom's business, like a town council, and they kept a tight hold on their land. But when it came to war, they were perfectly willing to give everyone a share in the fighting.

Noblemen no longer rode to battle in chariots and fought in single combat. Battles were now fought by long lines of men who formed a deadly wall of swords and shields. All armies used the new formation, and to be effective it required every man in the kingdom.

That meant more problems for the king. The citizen-soldiers began to ask why, if they were so important in battle, they should not be just as important at home. They made angry speeches at the Citizens' Assembly, to which all the men of the kingdom belonged. The Assembly had always had the right to vote on peace or war, but the citizens began to demand the right to vote on other things. They wanted land, new laws, more food, and lower taxes. The king promised to see what he could do, hoping that this would be enough to satisfy them.

REVOLT IN THE TOWNS

But the people were not so easily satisfied. Living in a town, they talked with their neighbors and the townsmen they met at the market. Soon they realized that together they were stronger than their ruler. They were ready for revolution, and all they needed was a leader.

In the little Greek kingdoms, there were many kings who wondered nervously what their people were saying when they met on the streets. Some rulers grew frightened and changed their laws to please the citizens. They were the ones who kept their thrones. Others waited until it was too late. Their own noblemen turned against them, drove them from their palaces, and set up councils to run the states. The councils of nobles, called oligarchies, were interested only in saving their own land and gold. In many states, they, too, were driven out—by men who won the people's trust.

GREEK TYRANTS

The new leaders ruled as tyrants. At first, the Greek word *tyrannos* meant no more than a leader who ruled alone and wrote his own laws. He might be good or bad. So many were bad that, in time, the meaning of the word changed and had no good in it. Meanwhile, the citizens' assemblies were growing stronger, and the people talked of running the government themselves. No nation had ever been governed that way, but the citizens of some cities decided to try it. These experiments led to democracy.

By 500 B.C., three hundred years after the Dark Age had ended, the Greeks had tried nearly every form of government that men could imagine. There were democracies, kingdoms, oligarchies, and cities ruled by tyrants. Each little country could choose its own kind of government, because it was separate and independent. No one thought of joining them to form one nation.

Foreigners could not understand it. Traveling around Greece, a foreigner met people who dressed alike, spoke the same language, traded with one another, and worshiped the same gods. In almost every way, they were like people who belonged to the same country. But when he asked them about the Greek nation, they laughed and said that there was no such thing. Their own city was a nation, they said; so was the city ten miles down the coast, and the one beyond that.

It was a puzzle—to everyone but the Greeks.

The key to the puzzle was the Greek word *polis*. A Greek would tell a foreigner that it meant "city"—at least, that was one of its meanings. A *polis* was a city and the fields outside its gates. It might include a mountain or two, a harbor, and sometimes several little country towns. So the foreigner tried calling it a "city-state," because it was more than a city, less than a country, and something like both.

THE VILLAGES OF GREECE WERE BUILT ON THE SLOPES OF HILLS, AT THE TOP OF WHICH ROSE A TEMPLE.

But the word meant more than that. *Polis* was also the government of the place. And *polis* meant the people, too—the people who were citizens, loyal to each other and to their own *polis*. The first of them had been tribesmen, who found an unclaimed valley or hilltop and took it as their own. The mountains and the ocean shut it off from the rest of the world, which was an advantage in the Dark Age. There were no good neighbors then. Any man who was not a member of the tribe was an enemy.

In three hundred years, a great city spread across the plain from the old stronghold on the acropolis. There were dozens of ships in its harbor, and its merchants sailed to every corner of the Mediterranean. But the land outside the *polis* was still foreign, and the men of the new cities were as loyal to their *polis* as the ancient warriors had been to their tribes. A citizen's *polis* was his home and the home of his gods. He had a place in its government, and it gave him his work, protection, and amusements.

THE *POLIS*

The Greeks said that a man who was not a citizen of a *polis* was nothing. A man who lived in an empire ruled by a king he had never seen was less than nothing—he was a slave. A man whose *polis* was defeated or destroyed might as well be dead. But the citizen whose *polis* was strong and free had everything. When he worked to make the best of his city and himself, he rivaled the gods in greatness. And that, the Greeks said, was the only reason for living.

The two most famous *poleis* (the plural of *polis*) reached greatness in different ways. Athens was a democracy, the home of politicians and artists, of merchants, scholars, and poets. The free men of the *polis* made it the richest and most beautiful city in Greece. Sparta, about 150 miles away by land, was a kingdom, and soldiering was its only interest. Its people lived on a military schedule; they almost thought together in platoons. Their *polis* was poor and plain, but without question it was the strongest city in the Greek world.

Athens: City of Wisdom and War

700 B.C.-500 B.C.

Of ALL the city-states in Greece, Athens was the most fortunate. The city's guardian was Athena, the goddess of war and wisdom. And, indeed, the Athenians did well in war and were blessed with wisdom. In the dark days, when barbaric invaders had conquered one city after another, Athens had not surrendered. Later, when Athens felt the growing pains that brought civil war and ruin to so many city-states, a series of wise men guided Athenians safely through their troubles. The right leaders always seemed to come along at the right time.

It was more than good luck, of course. The Athenians put their trust in men with new ideas, and they were willing to experiment. The experiments changed an ordinary little town into a great and brilliant *polis* that left an enduring mark on the world.

Athens was old. Its story began with a list of kings so ancient that no one was quite sure when they had lived. The greatest of them was Theseus, the young hero who killed the monster at Crete. The storytellers said that he won the friendship of the neighboring tribesmen and persuaded their

ATHENIANS WERE SHOCKED BY THE STRICT
LAWS OF DRACO, WHICH WERE INSCRIBED
ON A WALL IN THE CITY.

chiefs to swear loyalty to his city. That was the
beginning of the *polis,* but many years passed
before it became important.

In the seventh century B.C., Athens was only
a second-rate, backwoods *polis.* Its kings could
do little more than dream of the glorious old
days when their forefathers had defended the
town's acropolis—the Athenians called it the
Rock—against the barbarians. Attica, the countryside around the old fortress on the Rock, was really
ruled by a quarrelsome lot of rival noblemen, the
chiefs of the clans. These barons ran their vast
estates like private kingdoms. They owned the
country villages, and all but owned the people in
them. They were constantly fighting one another,
and often they set fire to a rival baron's fields,
destroying a year's crops in one day.

Something had to be done, for the endless
little wars were driving Athens to starvation and
ruin. The barons decided to change their ways.
They joined forces, captured the Rock, and set
up a council to help govern the *polis.* They swore
again the ancient oaths of loyalty to Athens and
prayed to Athena to teach them to live together in
peace.

But the old quarrels did not die so easily, and
new feuds broke out. The barons made life
miserable for the common people, who hated
them. And the people themselves were divided.
Those in the city and on the nearby farms, who
called themselves "The Plain," did not trust those
by the sea, who called themselves "The Coast."

To make things even worse, Athens had no
written laws. The council of judges, the *Areop-
agus,* was a committee of barons, and they
changed the laws to suit themselves. When a
baron claimed the land of a farmer who owed him
money, the council always ruled in favor of the
baron. If this still did not cover the debt, the
council gave the baron permission to sell the
farmer into slavery.

It happened that Athens had just begun to
trade with money instead of exchanging goods.
The barons were selling their crops abroad for
cash, and at home food became scarce. As prices
went up, the farmers had to borrow to live. More
and more of them lost their lands and their
freedom.

The people demanded laws to protect them,
laws that would not be changed from one day to
the next. In 621 B.C., the barons finally chose a
man named Draco to write a code of laws for the
city. But when the laws were posted, the citizens
who rushed to read them turned away angrily.
"Draco did not write these laws in ink!" they
shouted. "He wrote them in blood!"

For Draco's laws were strict, his punishments
harsh. Even the theft of a fig from a baron's
orchard meant death. Draco was asked if he
thought it was fair to give the same punishment
to petty thieves and murderers. He answered,
"Death is the proper punishment for a thief. It
is unfortunate that nature has not given us a
harsher one for a greater criminal."

SOLON THE WISE

After that, the people talked no more about
laws. They talked about war against the barons.
Both the people and the barons looked for a
general to lead them, and both turned to the same
man—Solon. The barons chose him because he
was a nobleman, a merchant's son who understood business and money. The people chose him
because he was a wise man, a poet who spoke out
against injustice and greed. Each side was sure
that he would fight for them, and each offered to
make him the tyrant of Athens.

Again the Athenians were lucky. Solon had
traveled widely and had seen for himself how
civil wars destroyed cities. He said he would not
be a tyrant or choose sides. If he could not work
with both sides, he would work with neither.
And if they wanted him at all, they must agree to
abide by the laws he made, whether they liked
them or not. The spokesmen for the two sides
looked at each other, nodded, and accepted his
terms.

In his first decree, Solon freed the farmers who
had been made slaves and forbade the selling of
citizens for their debts. He limited the amount
of land that one man could own, so that the
barons had to stop collecting little farms. Then
he canceled Draco's laws and wrote a new code
for Athens. When his laws were posted—first on
wooden tablets, then on stone columns set up in
the center of the city—no one shouted that they
were written in blood. The laws were sensible and
fair. They set up a Council of Four Hundred to
guide the city and watch over the judges. Any

117

citizen could be elected to the Council, and every citizen had the right to vote in the Assembly.

PISISTRATUS

Solon seemed to have thought of everything. There was a law that made it easier for poor farmers to plant profitable crops; a law that granted citizenship to foreign craftsmen who brought their businesses and families to Athens; a law that required every father to teach his son a trade. Competition among the men for rich wives was discouraged by a law that forbade a bride to have a dowry of more than three outfits of clothing and her kitchen pots. Another law said that ladies must not go out at night except in a chariot and with a torchbearer running ahead. And any man whose dog bit another man was ordered by law to deliver the animal to the magistrates with a log, four and a half feet long, tied to its neck.

When his work was done, Solon left Athens for ten years. He wanted the Athenians to see that his laws would work for them whether he was in the city or not. His cousin, Pisistratus, had other ideas—he planned to make himself tyrant of Athens. He felt that his chances were good. He had become a hero when he led the armies that won the island of Salamis for Athens. Since then he had made a great point of speaking well of the common people, which added to his popularity. There were still a number of people who hated the barons. Besides, some day the clans of the Plain and the Coast would start to quarrel again. And a new group had sprung up, the hill people. They were poor, they belonged to neither the Coast nor the Plain, they despised the barons, and they needed a leader. The time would surely come when Pisistratus would be able to take advantage of these divisions and dissatisfactions; meanwhile, he waited.

He waited for ten years. Solon returned to Athens, but he avoided politics, and Pisistratus saw no reason to change his own plans. Just as he had foreseen, the clansmen were at it again. Megacles, the leader of the Coast, had insulted Lycurgus, the leader of the Plain. The people of the hills were now well organized and called themselves "The Hill." Pisistratus thought most of them were rather stupid, but he needed them for fighting, not for thinking.

In 561 B.C., Pisistratus believed the time had come for him to act. One morning he raced his

chariot into the crowded market place. As he reined his winded horses to a halt, the people saw that he was wounded. Staggering from the chariot, he pointed to his wounds and gasped, "I have these because I spoke for the people!"

As a matter of fact, Pisistratus had made the wounds himself. They were shallow cuts, the kind that bleed a great deal but heal quickly. The people did not know that, of course. They called for a special meeting of the Assembly, where they demanded protection for Pisistratus. Solon, who saw through his cousin's trick, tried to tell the people the truth. They were too excited to listen, and he lost his temper. "You are each so clever," he cried. "How can you be so stupid when you get together?"

Stupid or not, the Assembly voted to give Pisistratus a bodyguard of fifty men with clubs. In the next few days, the bodyguard grew until it numbered close to a hundred men. They marched on the Acropolis, and the hill people poured into the city to join the fight. The Acropolis was taken, and suddenly Pisistratus was tyrant of Athens.

ATHEN'S NEW TYRANT

The barons who led the men of the Plain and the Coast patched up their quarrels and rushed to attack the Hill. Pisistratus was driven out, but the barons fell to arguing among themselves again. Megacles of the Coast became so angry that he switched sides and offered to help Pisistratus. There was one condition, however—Pisistratus must marry his daughter.

Pisistratus agreed, and the two men worked out a wild scheme. The Greek historian Herodotus described it in this way:

"They put together the most ridiculous scheme that I imagine was ever thought of. I say that, first, because the Greeks have always been famous for their shrewdness; and, second, because this trick was played on the Athenians, who are always said to be the cleverest of all the Greeks. They found a woman called Phye (which means 'tall') who was nearly six feet tall and very beautiful, too. They dressed her in a suit of armor, rehearsed her in the part she was to play, and drove into the city. There the heralds, who had been sent ahead, cried, 'Men of Athens, give kind welcome to Pisistratus. Athena honors him above all other men and has come to bring him to her own Acropolis.' They shouted this about the city, and the people, sure that the woman was the goddess, took back Pisistratus and paid worship to a girl from the country."

THE GREEK FOOT SOLDIERS, ARMED WITH SPEARS AND WITH SHIELDS FOR PROTECTION, WERE CALLED HOPLITES.

THE TYRANT PISISTRATUS ADDRESSING A CROWD OF ATHENIANS

Herodotus did not say what Solon did this time. Perhaps he simply stayed home in disgust. In any case, Pisistratus was tyrant again, but only for two years. When he married Megacles' daughter, he refused to treat her as his wife or to pay any attention to her at all. Megacles was furious. He wanted to be the father-in-law of a tyrant, and had hoped to be the grandfather of another. Instead, he and his daughter had been insulted. He promptly organized Pisistratus' old enemies, the clans and the barons, and chased him out of Athens.

For twelve years, Pisistratus stayed away. But he was never without a scheme, and he made good use of the time. He toured the Mediterranean collecting a few unclaimed islands and dropping in on any city where the ruler was willing to welcome him. Then, while he was in Macedonia, he got hold of a gold mine. With the profits of the mine he bought an army, and in 544 B.C. he was back in Athens and became tyrant again. When the barons took a good look at his army, most of them decided to leave the *polis* in a hurry. So did Megacles, and none of them came back while Pisistratus lived. He was finally able to rule Athens, and even Solon said that, for a tyrant, he did a good job.

For the citizens, it was a fine time. Under Solon's laws, their little country had grown up. The new shopping district around the market square had become the meeting place of people from every corner of the Mediterranean world. The Athenians, whose grandparents had known only the village gossip of Attica, now talked Egyptian politics, read poetry from Rhodes, and told the latest jokes from Syracuse almost as soon as the Syracusans did. But Pisistratus was still not satisfied.

Solon had brought craftsmen and merchants to Athens. Pisistratus wanted builders and poets, anyone who could give the *polis* beauty and fame. He announced to all the world that once every four years the Panathenaean Festival, the city's greatest holiday, would include international games and contests. The citizens of every Greek city were invited to enter. Competitors and spectators flocked to Athens, for no Greek could resist a good contest.

THE ATHENIAN GAMES

On the first three days of the festival, athletes competed in races and wrestling. There was a contest, too, for the *rhapsodes*, the minstrels who sang the tales of Homer. On the fourth day, the winners of all the contests joined the great procession of Athenians that wound its way through the city and up the Acropolis to the temple of the goddess. A tall model of a ship on wheels led the parade. On its mast was fastened a magnificent robe which the maidens of the city had woven for Athena. Following the ship rode charioteers and horsemen of the Athenian cavalry. Then came the elders of the city, musicians playing on pipes and lyres, and youths leading the animals for sacrifice. Dancers with clicking castanets wove in and out of the long train of marchers. When the procession reached the temple, the maidens put the splendid robe around the shoulders of the statue of the goddess. The animals were sacrificed at the altar, and a hush fell over the people while every man made his prayer to Athena, asking her to remember her city. Then, shouting and singing, the crowd rushed down the hill to the victory feasts and the dancing that would end the festival.

The men who came to compete in the games went home talking about the splendors of Athens, and Pisistratus saw to it that there was more for them to talk about each time they returned. He had the old wooden temples on the Acropolis rebuilt in fine white stone. Perhaps he hoped that the gods would forgive him for once having made the Athenians kneel before a false Athena. He ordered a new temple for Dionysus, the god of wine and crops. When it was finished, he proclaimed another festival, the Great Dionysia of the City, a celebration that brought about one of the Greeks' greatest experiments.

The Great Dionysia was held in early spring, when the grapevines had just begun to sprout. For five days, all work stopped in Athens, while the city celebrated the end of winter. The people feasted together and toasted each other with glass after glass of wine. There was singing and dancing around the altar of the new temple.

In the old days, the singers had worn goatskins in order to look like Dionysus' servants, the satyrs. It was said that satyrs were half men and half beasts, with pointed ears and tails like horses. Their chants were "goat-songs"—noisy, braying hymns for a god who liked to laugh. But Pisistratus had decided to add a contest to this festival, too—a contest for new songs. Instead of goat-songs, the musicians and poets brought songs about other gods and, of course, the heroes in Homer. The chorus at the temple changed their goatskins for costumes that went with the stories. Then the chorus leaders began to sing some of the lines as solos, to make the tales clearer and more exciting.

One day, the people who had come to watch the song contest suddenly sat up in surprise. Something odd was happening. The leader had just begun his solo. But instead of telling a story about a man, he spoke as if he were that man himself. He talked to the chorus as though they were friends he had just run into on the street. It was strange.

The audience had never heard of acting or of plays. Until that afternoon, there had never been a play at all. But when it came time to choose the winner of the song contest, the crowd voted to give the prize to Thespis, the man who had written the odd new poem. Pisistratus, delighted, announced a new contest—for plays.

Not everyone agreed that Thespis' idea was a good one. After that first play, Solon told Thespis that a man pretending to be someone else had to lie to do it. Wasn't Thespis ashamed to ask a man to tell lies, especially in front of so many people? Thespis answered that there was no harm in it, because the man was playing. Solon struck his staff on the ground angrily. "If we honor that sort of thing in play," he said, "some day we will find it happening in our business!"

The younger Athenians were willing to take that risk. They hurried to see more plays, and built a grandstand beside the clearing in front of the temple where the performances were given— the first theater.

Meanwhile, Pisistratus was busy with new projects. He had two great dreams. The first was to build a temple for Zeus that would be bigger and more magnificent than any other temple in Greece. The other was to have his sons and his sons' sons rule the *polis.* Perhaps his dreams were too ambitious. Or perhaps, as many people said, Athena had not forgiven him. Both of his projects failed. When he died in 528 B.C., work stopped at his mammoth temple, and no Athenian ever tried to finish it. His sons, Hippias and Hipparchus, did rule Athens for a while. Then Hipparchus was killed in a quarrel, and the citizens sided with his murderers. Tyrant or not, they said, he was in the wrong. Hippias overheard their complaints. Fearing for his own life, he turned harsh and cruel. The people grew angrier, and the barons, who had fled when Pisistratus marched his army into Athens, decided it was time to come home again.

One noble family, the rich and powerful Alcmoenids, had long been plotting the downfall of Pisistratus and his sons. But they had waited for Athens to grow weary of tyrants, and for the help of soldiers from Sparta. Now Athens was sick of Hippias. It was time for the Spartans to step in, and the Alcmoenids knew just how to manage that.

Because they were famous for sharp trading and getting the most for the money, the Alcmoenids had won the contract to build a great new Temple of Apollo at Delphi. Delphi was the place of the Oracle, who gave advice to the rulers of every *polis* in Greece. The Oracle's message came from the gods, but only the priests could understand it, so it was up to them to tell the kings and statesmen what the gods were saying. It was also up to them to worry about the cost of the new building and how it would look. The plans called for good, white stone, but not the best; that would be too expensive. But the Alcmoenids used the hardest, finest stone obtainable, and they paid the difference themselves. The priests were delighted and very grateful. The Alcmoenids said they were happy to give Apollo

WORSHIPERS BROUGHT OFFERINGS TO THE TEMPLE OF APOLLO AT DELPHI.

a good home, even though they could not enjoy their own homes at Athens unless the Spartans agreed to fight Hippias. Somehow, after that, whenever the kings of Sparta came to ask the Oracle for advice—whether the question was about starting a war or planting crops—the answer the priests gave them was always: "Free Athens first!"

The Spartans were not eager to fight, but it was hard to ignore the advice of the gods. They finally agreed to help the Alcmoenids and the other noblemen, and together they marched on Athens. Hippias and his followers locked themselves inside the walls of the Acropolis. For several days they held off the attackers. Then the Spartans captured Hippias' children and the tyrant surrendered. He left the city, promising never to return.

Athens was free, but not peaceful. When the noblemen trooped back to Attica to claim their old estates, the people went to war to stop them. The Coast, the Plain, and the Hill began to quarrel again, then joined in the fighting. The bewildered Spartans decided to let Athens save itself and went home. It seemed to them that the Athenians would go on quarreling until they destroyed each other and their *polis*. But they did not know Athens. Once again, there was a man with an idea—Cleisthenes.

Cleisthenes was an Alcmoenid, the leader of the noblemen, but he was an Athenian first. His plan for a new kind of government for Athens was one which he hoped would put a stop to the feuds and make a good life possible for nobles and commoners alike. When he explained the plan to the Athenians, they agreed to make the experiment. It meant making many changes, but almost anything would be better than the constant wars.

First, Cleisthenes divided the citizens into ten new clans. Each had the same vote in the city council, and each was made up of equal numbers of people from the Plain, the Coast, and the Hill. Old enemies were forced to become allies, and the feuding stopped.

There was still the danger that a proud man like Pisistratus might try to become a tyrant. But Cleisthenes had an answer for that, too—a backward sort of election, called "the ostracism." Once a year all the citizens were called together in the market place, and each man was given a clay ballot on which he could write the name of a politician who seemed dangerously eager to be important. The ballots were dropped into huge clay jars, one for each clan. Then the officials emptied the jars, threw away the blank ballots, and counted the ones with names written on them. To make the election legal, at least 6,000 ballots had to be cast. The man who got the most votes had to leave Athens for ten years. Suddenly there were few men who wanted to be tyrant.

Now Cleisthenes tried his greatest experiment.

122

He said that every official of the *polis*—the councilmen, judges, and planners—would be chosen by the votes of the people. Even the ten generals would be elected, one from each of the new clans. Any citizen could be named.

DEMOCRACY INVENTED

The Athenians, pleased with the system that gave every citizen a place in the government, did their best to make the plan work. The old quarrels began to be forgotten, and the experiment was a success. Cleisthenes had invented democracy.

Athens had moved with amazing speed. All the changes, from Draco's harsh laws to the new democracy, had been made in less than 100 years. But there were some things that remained the same, and one of them was slavery. Prisoners of war, especially barbarians, were sold as slaves in every Greek city. There were many of them in Athens—a few on the farms, some in the mines, and the rest in the city. Most families kept one or two as cooks, cleaners, or nursemaids. Craftsmen used them as helpers in their workshops. Often they worked side by side with free men, doing the same jobs. In some cities, slaves were treated with savage cruelty, but in Athens they had a better time of it, and there were laws to curb the harshness of bad-tempered masters. The Spartans joked about that. They said that when you met an Athenian and his slave in the street, you could not tell the difference between them.

The Athenians, however, knew that there was a difference. A slave was a man who had so little pride that he let himself be captured, giving up his honor to save his skin. It was wrong to treat him cruelly, but he did not deserve to be free.

Not that being free guaranteed anyone the vote. The foreign merchants and craftsmen who came to live in Athens were free men, but many of them stayed for years without being given the rights of citizenship. Though the Athenians were happy to have them do business, they were still suspicious of strangers and in no hurry to let them vote.

No woman could vote, not even if she was a native of Athens. According to an old story, women as well as men had once belonged to the Assembly. Then there was an argument about which of the gods should be the special guardian of the city. Some citizens wanted Athena, a goddess. Others preferred Poseidon, a god who was a man and a warrior. When it came to a vote in the Assembly, all the men voted for the god and all the women voted for the goddess. Since there were more women than men at the meeting, Athena was elected. But the men had their revenge. At the first meeting where they outnumbered the women, they voted them out of the Assembly altogether.

Probably it was just a story. Nevertheless, Athens was a man's democracy and a man's city. Women were not expected to go about the streets freely. Their place was at home. Girls spent their time learning to be good wives for citizens, not to be citizens themselves. While they waited for their fathers to come to terms with the men who asked to marry them, they kept busy with ladylike activities: cooking, weaving, and especially spinning. The girls who waited too long for marriage were called "spinsters."

Foreigners sometimes thought that Athenian women must be dull and uneducated. That was because foreigners had almost no chance to meet them. And few foreigners had not heard about the Athenian who boasted that his new wife had been brought up to "see as little, hear as little, and ask as few questions as possible." But most citizens wanted wives who were cleverer than that. It was true that a woman had little or no chance to see the world, but she heard about it from her husband. He was her teacher, and he expected her to be bright enough to keep up with the things that interested him. He brought her the latest poems and books, discussed politics with her, and at festival time he took her with him to the ceremonies and the contests. If an Athenian wife was dull, she probably had a dull husband.

There was little excuse, however, for an Athenian to be dull. He grew up in the most exciting city in Greece and, unlike his sisters, he was always in the midst of things. At his birth, his family had celebrated because he was a boy, a future citizen. They spent all that they could afford to train him for his most important job, serving Athens. For six or seven years the little boy was pampered by his nursemaid. She saw to it that his bed was soft and his food the best in the house. She kept a careful eye on him when he rode around the courtyard in his little goat cart.

Then it was time for school. Instead of a nursemaid, the boy was looked after by a pedagogue, a slave who carried his books, guarded him in the streets, and made certain that he got to school on time. Classes began early. The student and his pedagogue left the house at dawn, just as the first farmers and tradesmen were hurrying to the market place. The school was in the house of the teacher, a poor man; but one who had had all the training of a citizen. In the mornings, the students practiced writing on wax tablets with sharp sticks of ivory. The sticks had a blunt end for "erasing" mistakes. When it was time for arithmetic, however, the sticks and tablets were usually put away. The Greek system for writing down numbers was awkward, and the boys often used pebbles instead. They called the pebbles *calculus,* and when they counted with them, they "calculated." The youngest boys had lessons in reading, as well as in writing and arithmetic, but reading was only for beginners. Older students learned by discussions and arguments, and by chanting verses from Homer and other great writers.

Music and poetry were most important studies, especially in Athens. Every well-bred Athenian man was expected to be able to play the flute or the lyre, an instrument like a small harp. For music was more than a pleasant way to fill an afternoon or evening. The songs told the stories of the heroes and the gods. They were tales of courage and wisdom, and from them the boys learned what was expected of citizens.

Not all of the lessons were taught in the classroom. For several hours each day, school was held in a wrestling academy, a gymnasium which the master owned or rented. There were games and exercises, and training in wrestling or boxing. The boys enviously watched the older athletes, who were getting ready for the international games, and they dreamed of the time when they could compete themselves. A healthy mind in a healthy body was the goal of every Athenian. He wanted to excel at everything—to be the best there was. It was the way to win the favor of the gods, and it was his duty to Athens.

When they were eighteen, the boys left school. Many of them went on studying, talking and arguing with the wise men who gathered in the market place. They swore the oath of citizenship, but were not yet full citizens. First they had to spend a year training with the army. At the end of that year came the moment for which they had been working all of their lives. On a day that was sacred to Athena and the *polis,* the young men marched together to the Acropolis. There the people of Athens waited to greet them. As they came to the top of the hill, near the temple of the goddess, the crowds hailed them as citizens, new men of Athens.

On that special day, when the proud young citizens gave themselves to their *polis,* no one could doubt that Athens was the most fortunate city in Greece.

SCENES FROM ATHENIAN LIFE: BLACKSMITHS AND SCULPTORS AT WORK; A TEACHER INSTRUCTS A PUPIL; A BANQUET.

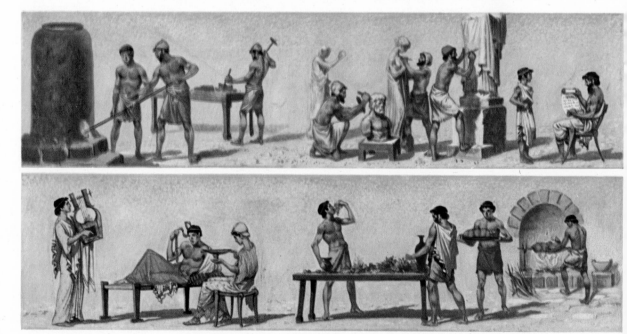

THE SPARTANS MARCHED OFF TO WAR TO THE SOUND OF FLUTES.

Sparta:
City of Soldiers

700 B.C.-500 B.C.

IN SPARTA, the shops in the market place had little gold or jewelry to sell, and no fine furniture at all. The people in the streets were not well dressed. Even the temples, although big, were plain, and there was little in Sparta to show that this was the strongest *polis* in Greece.

Sparta was old-fashioned and proud of it. The *polis* had begun as a kingdom, and it stayed a kingdom. The only change its citizens made in more than 400 years was to have two kings instead of one. Each kept a watchful eye on the other, and the one who was the better general took charge of the army.

For a Spartan, that was progress enough. He did not like experiments. The system that modern Athens called "democracy" looked to him like bad organization, and if there was one thing a Spartan wanted it was to keep things in order. His own days and years were run on a strict military schedule, because he was a soldier in the army. Each citizen of the *polis* was in the army. He started his training when he was seven and he remained a soldier until he was sixty. His orders came from his officers, the kings, and the five *ephors* who managed the day-to-day affairs of the city. He obeyed orders and had no time for experimenting with newfangled ideas.

In the early days, Sparta had been very much like Athens. But in the seventh century B.C., when Athens was changing almost from day to day, the Spartans established their own way of doing things. As a matter of fact, they had no choice. Their ancestors, a fierce tribe of Dorian invaders, had taken the city from its old Achaean rulers. Using iron swords, they had quickly overrun the neighboring kingdoms. By the time they stopped, they had conquered the entire southern half of the Peloponnesus. This gave them much land, as well as the serfs they needed to work on the land. But it gave them trouble, too, because there were many more serfs than Spartans.

In the seventh century, the serfs, who were

called *helots,* rose up against their masters. It took every citizen to hold off the furious mobs that attacked with clubs and sticks and broken hoes. During the long fight against the serfs, the city was turned into a military camp. The people lived in barracks and ate in public mess halls. Comforts were forgotten. There was no time for anything that did not help to win the war. When at last the *helots* were beaten down, the Spartans did not dare to put away their arms. They knew that at the first sign of weakness the *helots* would be at their throats again. So Sparta remained a city of soldiers standing watch over its serfs.

The big army, always in top fighting condition, began to worry the rulers of nearby *poleis.* Their own troops were not nearly so strong. Then it occurred to them that the Spartans might be willing to lend a hand when a neighbor was in trouble. The Spartans were willing, so long as the others agreed to let them decide where and how the battles would be fought. One by one, their neighbors came to terms. By the sixth cen-

tury, all but two of the cities of the Peloponnesus had put their troops under Spartan command, and Sparta was on call to defend half of Greece.

At home, serfs did the farm work and foreigners were the city's only craftsmen and merchants. No one was rich, but that was a part of the Spartan plan. It was covered by their strict laws, which had been written by an ancient king named Lycurgus. No one remembered exactly who he was or where he had come from. People simply said he was a relative of the gods and let it go at that. But when they talked about law, they were always careful to say, "Lycurgus said . . ."

Lycurgus had believed that rich citizens would be tempted to disobey their officers. For that reason, citizens were not allowed to go into business, and they gave up their gold and silver coins for money made of iron. The new money would not buy much and a fortune in iron was useless. It took a big cupboard to hold a hundred dollars worth of iron bars, and an ox cart to move them. In fact, the only handy thing about them was that they were completely safe from robbers.

SPARTANS LINED THE STREETS TO CHEER THE PROCESSION OF THEIR VICTORIOUS ARMY.

Anyway, Spartans had little use for money. Luxuries were against the law, because they made men soft. The *polis* furnished its citizens with necessities. Lycurgus had laid down the law on almost everything that could happen in the life of a man. At birth, an official decided if the baby looked healthy enough to be allowed to live. At death, another official decided how many people could go to the funeral. In between, there was the army.

At the age of seven, the boys left their homes and began training. Every lesson was meant to toughen them up. Summer and winter, they went barefoot and wore light clothes. Exercises made them strong and fast, but not until the time of the Peloponnesian Wars did Sparta allow the athletic contests that the other Greeks loved. Soldiers who tried to outdo each other, Lycurgus said, became rivals instead of a team. The greatest Spartan contest was a public whipping; the winner was the boy who took the worst beating without a cry.

EVENING IN SPARTA

When the boys came to their mess halls after a long day of marching and exercises, they found little food on the tables. Lycurgus said that thin children grew up, not out. Besides, the boys were expected to steal enough food to fill their stomachs—that was how soldiers lived in the field. Young Spartans were not punished for stealing, but for being caught at it.

In the evenings, there was music, the one Spartan art. It was all right for a boy to learn to play the flute, because the army marched into battle to the piping of flutes. The songs were rousing choruses and ballads about victorious heroes, the kind of songs that were good for cheering tired soldiers. When it was time for sleep, the boys made their beds of rushes, breaking the tough stems with their hands because there was a rule against cutting them with a knife. In cold weather, they added thistledown for a little warmth. And if their beds were neither soft nor warm, they were too tired to care.

At twenty, the young Spartans went into the regular army. They could marry then, but they still had to live in their barracks. They were not allowed to have their own homes until they turned thirty, the age at which they officially became men. Even then, however, they took their meals with the army, because Lycurgus said that all men should eat together, sharing the same bread and meat. Along Hyacinthian Street, in the middle of the city, stood the rows of mess tents. Each was a club for fifteen soldiers. A club picked its own members, and no one was allowed to join unless all the members voted to invite him. Choosing the right men was important, because the clubs not only ate together, but fought together when the army went to war. When they were in Sparta, each man was expected to contribute a certain amount of food every month: a bushel of wheat, five pounds of cheese, two and a half pounds of figs, eight gallons of wine, and a little money. The money bought meat for the famous "black broth" that kept the Spartans strong and jolted the stomachs of most other Greeks who tried to swallow it.

After the meal, the men went to their houses, finding their way along the streets without torches—that was good practice for marching in the dark. At home, their wives and daughters would already have eaten. They had more time to themselves than the men did, and they were not shut up in their houses like the Athenian women. Their tongues were free, too. It was an old joke in Greece that Spartan men were made tough by the harsh words of their women.

There was another Greek story, however, about the Spartan mother's farewell to her son before his first battle. Other women might weep and pray for their sons to come home safe, but Spartan mothers only said, "Return with your shield or be carried dead upon it."

Most Greeks believed that story. If they smiled at the Spartan's rude and narrow way of life, they never laughed at his prowess in battle. His speech was short, his comforts few, but soldiering was his trade and fighting was his art. He would never bring shame to himself or to his *polis* by dropping his shield and running. He would stand his ground or be killed.

The one time that Spartans allowed themselves to be elegant was in battle. When the flutes began to play, they marched toward the field as though they were marching to a party. Their bodies were rubbed with perfumed oil. They wore their richest armor, the one expensive thing they owned. Their long hair was curled and decked with garlands of flowers. If a man was the best soldier in the world, they thought, he ought to look it. As Lycurgus said, "A fine head of hair adds beauty to a handsome face, and terror to an ugly one."

Greece Fights for Its Life

499 B.C.-479 B.C.

ACROSS the Aegean, from the oriental court of King Darius of Persia, came messengers to all the city-states of mainland Greece. Their words were smooth, their smiles like sneers, and they demanded gifts for their master—earth and water, the ancient tokens of tribute and surrender.

The Greeks in Asia Minor already knew the Persians—too well. Once the smiling messengers had come to their cities. After the messengers, the soldiers came, attacking the little *poleis,* one by one, until all of them were taken. Nothing could stop the Persian armies. From their capital, deep in Asia, they had pushed westward, and they had gone so far that the journey home was counted in months instead of miles. They had conquered Egypt and Phoenicia, the kingdom of sailors. Now Darius, their king, meant to add Greece to his empire. He would do it quietly, if the Greeks gave up without a fight. If not, he would send his soldiers and take Greece by force.

When the messengers arrived, the men of some *poleis* bowed their heads and gave the tokens; if Darius came, they would not fight. Others refused. The Spartans dropped the Persian ambassadors down a well and told them to find their earth and water there. At Athens, Darius' messengers were thrown into a pit.

Darius was not sorry that the Athenians were so bold. He had a grudge to settle with them, and he looked forward to seeing his troops destroy their city. Seven years before, in 499 B.C., Athens and Eretria, another city on the mainland, had sent help to the Greeks in Asia Minor. When Darius was told about it, he had sneered, "The Athenians—who are they?" He had called for his bow and an arrow, which he shot toward the heavens. It was his message to the gods, asking

BOW OF A TRIREME, THE SHIP USED AGAINST THE PERSIANS

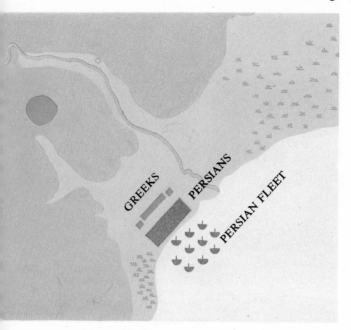

THE BATTLE AT MARATHON

them to let him punish Athens. Then he commanded his servant to say to him three times each day, "Sire, remember the Athenians."

Herodotus, the historian, told the story when he wrote about the three times that the kings of Persia tried to conquer the Greeks. The luck of Athens had never met so harsh a test before. When the greatest army in the world picked Greece to be the next victim, only Sparta, out of all the city-states, was ready to defend itself.

Nature saved the Greeks from the first attack. The Persian fleet sailed close to the rocky coast, keeping watch over Darius' army, which was moving by land. A storm blew up and smashed the ships against the shore, and the expedition had to turn back. Two years later, in 490 B.C., the Persians tried again. This time they carried their soldiers on the ships and sailed straight across the Aegean to Eretria. They took the city, burned it to the ground, and then crossed the narrow channel to Marathon on the coast of Attica. Athens was just a good day's march away.

The Athenians sent their fastest runner, Pheidippides, to Sparta to ask for help. He ran as no man had run before. Not once did he stop to rest, and he made the 150-mile journey in two days. When he returned to Athens, he said that the god Pan had appeared to him along the road. Pan had promised to help the Athenians if they would remember to honor him in their city. It

was a good omen, but the news from Sparta was bad. The Spartan troops were willing to come, but a law of their religion said that they could not leave until the full moon had shone, and that would not be for several days.

The Athenian Assembly was in an uproar when it met. Five of the city's ten generals urged the people to vote to keep the army in the city until the Persians attacked. The other five, however, wanted to meet the invaders at Marathon. Miltiades, the officer in charge of planning Athens' campaigns, managed to make himself heard above the noise. He was in favor of the march to Marathon. But the five generals still disagreed. If the army went to Marathon and was defeated, they said, there would be no one left to defend the city. It was safer to keep the soldiers inside the walls.

Miltiades spoke again. He told the citizens that Hippias, their old tyrant, was with the Persian commanders. Were they willing to hide like cowards behind their walls, he asked, while Hippias waited for them to starve and surrender? The Athenians' anger began to get the better of their fear. When the Assembly voted, it ordered the generals to go to Marathon to fight.

THE BATTLE OF MARATHON

The plain of Marathon stretched along a curving beach edged with mountains. The Persians had made their camp between the beach, where their boats were moored, and a rushing stream, which split the plain in two. The Athenians set up their camp in a little valley just above. It was a perfect position. The mountains protected the valley, and no army, no matter how large, could attack it successfully. The Athenians could sit there safely for weeks, and every day that passed brought the full moon and the Spartans that much closer. The Persians, on the other hand, had to move fast. Moreover, there were only two roads by which they could reach Athens. One of them was cut off by the Athenian camp. To get to the other, the Persians would have to march across the plain, and the Athenians would pour out of the valley and attack the side of their columns.

For several days, the armies sat in their camps. Then the Persian commander, who had 30,000 men or more to Athens' 10,000, decided to risk the march. As the long column moved across the plain, the men in the valley charged out to attack it. The soldiers in the column turned and the armies met face to face, like the lines of two enormous football teams. Advancing behind their tall wicker shields, the Persians pushed the Athenian center farther and farther back. But on the wings, the Persians were forced to retreat. The Athenian generals had deliberately left their center weak and put all their strength at the end of the line. When the Persian wings broke and the soldiers ran for the ships, the strong Athenian wings turned and closed in. Suddenly the Persians who were fighting at the center were trapped. They scattered, dropped their arms, and fled. Many were caught along the beach, for the Persian ships were already pulling away, leaving their dead and wounded behind. For a day or two, the fleet hovered off the shore of Attica. Then it turned away and sailed for home, taking Hippias back to Asia.

Meanwhile, the Athenians had lit the bonfire that signaled victory, and had counted dead on the field—192 men of Athens, 6,400 Persians. The Spartans arrived, in good time for the celebration, but too late to fight. For the men of Athens, that made it a double victory. The god Pan, who had helped the Athenians, was given a new shrine near the Acropolis. Every year, on the anniversary of the battle, a race was run to honor him and Pheidippides, the man who had run 150 miles in two days. Wherever the story was told, the contests that tested the strength of athletes in long-distance runs began to be called marathon races.

Many Greeks thought that Marathon had ended the wars with Persia. In Athens, however, there was a young politician who insisted that it was no more than a beginning. He begged the people and the generals to get ready for the battles he was sure would come. Older, more powerful statesmen disagreed with him. They said that this noisy young man, Themistocles, was just trying to make a name for himself by frightening the city. They reminded the people that Themistocles was only half Athenian—his mother came from a different *polis*. They said Themistocles was a show-off, always too eager to get up and talk in the Assembly, always richly dressed. That sort of thing was not Athenian, they said. If the people wanted to vote for Themistocles, they should wait until the ostracism and vote for him to leave the *polis*.

However, the citizens knew Themistocles as the one important man who called them by name when he met them on the street. When he was a judge, they could trust him to decide things fairly. If he was so worried about the Per-

sians, they thought, there must be a reason for it. When the election for ostracism was held, they voted for his enemies to leave Athens. After that, Themistocles was free to go ahead with his plans for making Athens strong. He persuaded the people to spend money from the state treasury for ships—dozen of *triremes*, the huge battleships that were manned by three ranks of rowers. He rebuilt the old harbor at Piraeus, five miles from the city. Sparta could rely on land forces, he said, but Athens must be a sea power. His ships could defeat the Persians before they came near Attica, and, in the meantime, they would help Athens to grow rich by trading.

But Athens alone could not defend all of Greece. Themistocles was angry when he saw how little the other cities were doing to get ready for the war. He called for them to prepare their defenses and to forget their old rivalries long enough to make plans together. For years, they ignored him and did nothing. Then, when it was nearly too late, the leaders of thirty-one *poleis* finally met together in a Greek congress. They decided to combine their troops into one great army under the command of Leonidas, one of the kings of Sparta. The Spartans demanded control of the fleet, too, though most of the ships were Athenian. Themistocles agreed, and for the time being the Greeks were united, busily preparing to meet the attack.

The Persians had spent ten years getting ready for the war. King Darius was dead, but Xerxes, the new king, had sworn to avenge the defeat at Marathon. Now the Persian troops and the armies of all the nations that they had conquered were waiting in Asia Minor. Squadron after squadron of warships sailed toward the Hellespont to join the Persian fleet. The sleek Phoenician battleships and the lumbering warships of Egypt were now under Xerxes' orders.

Meanwhile, Xerxes' generals tried to line up the armies. There were so many men that they had trouble simply counting them. Finally, they counted off 10,000 soldiers, crowded them together in a field, set up a wall around them, then emptied the field. Then they marched the rest of the troops through the field, one group after another. Each time the space inside the walls was filled, they checked off another 10,000.

No one knows just how many times the space was emptied and filled again. The Greek historian Herodotus said it was one hundred and seventy times—a total of 1,700,000 foot soldiers. But

THE PERSIAN ARMY CROSSED THE HELLESPONT ON A BRIDGE BUILT OF BOATS.

when Herodotus wrote his history, nearly half a century after the war, he used the figures the old soldiers remembered. Probably there were less than half that number of foot soldiers. Even so, with cavalry, sailors, marines, officers, attendants, grooms, cooks, and the rest, the force that Xerxes called together to attack Greece was the most gigantic military machine that the Mediterranean world had ever known.

Xerxes gave the order to march. Rowers pulled at their oars, the cavalrymen spurred their horses, and the infantrymen marched to the Hellespont and stopped. The bridges built to carry them across the water had been washed away by a storm, and Xerxes bellowed with rage. He ordered his men to give the waves three hundred lashes while they shouted: "Treacherous river, Xerxes the king will cross you, with or without your permission!"

A string of boats was lashed together to make a new bridge and the armies of Xerxes walked across the Hellespont. In the lead were the Persian foot soldiers in coats of mail, with their tall bows slung across their shoulders. Behind them stretched a strange, long parade, the men of forty-six nations in the war gear of their homelands—

cotton-clad Indians, and Caspians in goatskins; Sarangians in elegant high boots and brilliantly colored cloaks; Sagartians, who lassoed their enemies and finished them off with daggers; the Sacae, who fought with axes; Thracians in foxskin caps and Colchians with cowskin shields; bronze-helmeted Assyrians, with lances and short swords; and Ethiopians, who wrapped themselves in the skins of leopards and lions, and still used arrowheads of stone. All of Asia marched against the Greeks. The war that was about to begin would be East against West, and to the winner would go Greece, the Aegaean, the Mediterranean, and perhaps the world.

In July, 480 B.C., the Persian armies, marching south through Thessaly, ran into the first strong Greek defense. The Spartan king, Leonidas, and a force of 7,000 men had blocked off Thermopylae, a narrow pass fenced in by mountains and the sea. It was the one place where a small Greek army could hope to hold off Xerxes' hordes. The ends of the pass were so narrow that only a few attackers could come through at a time, and they would be easy targets for the Spartan spearmen. The only way around the pass was a steep mountain trail. The Persians probably did not know of it, but, taking no chances, Leonidas had it guarded by 1,000 men.

Meanwhile, the Greek fleet had moved up to meet the Persian ships that always followed Xerxes along the coast. A lucky storm and a daring raid by an Athenian squadron delayed the Persian fleet. Now it was up to the men at Thermopylae to stop the army. Xerxes came to the west end of the pass, and for four days he waited. On the fifth day, he attacked, but the Greek spears drove his men back. He tried again the next day, and again he failed. But he found a Greek named Epialtes who was willing to show him the way through the mountains. The traitor and a troop of Persians scrambled to the top of the path, and the men who had been sent to defend it dropped their arms and fled.

THE BATTLE OF THERMOPYLAE

When Leonidas was told what had happened, he sent half of his men away to safety. But he and the best of his Spartans stayed where they were, determined to hold off the Persians. In the morning, Xerxes' troops attacked both ends of the pass. By nightfall, every Greek at Thermopylae was dead, and Xerxes gave his Persians the order to march on toward Attica.

Fear swept Athens. The Spartan generals had pulled back the Greek armies to the Isthmus, the shoestring of land at the top of the Peloponnesus. The Isthmus was an easy place to defend, they said, and it protected Sparta—but Athens was left defenseless. The leaders of the city hurried to Delphi to ask the Oracle for the advice of the gods. The Oracle's reply was terrible: "All is ruined, for fire and the headlong God of War speeding in a Syrian chariot shall bring you low."

The whole city prayed to Athena, begging her to ask Zeus for some promise of hope. The Oracle spoke again: "The wooden wall shall not fall, but will help you and your children." The message was puzzling, but Themistocles saw its meaning. The wooden wall was a barricade of ships, he said, and the Athenians must go to a place where their ships could protect them. He urged them to flee to the island of Salamis. The Greek fleet was already moored in the bay between the island and the coast of Attica, and he promised that, no matter what the Spartans wanted, the ships would remain there.

The people did not want to leave Athens, but Themistocles said that he knew no other way to save them. So they gathered up the few things they could carry, took a last sad look at their homes and the temples on the Rock, and boarded the boats that would take them to Salamis. Behind them, the great city fell silent, except for the dogs that ran through the streets, howling for their masters.

On September 17, the Persians entered the city. Only the Acropolis was guarded. There a little band of soldiers and priests held off the attackers, rolling stones on them from the top of the hill. But after two weeks, the Acropolis was taken and Athens was burned.

VICTORY AT SALAMIS

Now the Spartans demanded that the fleet be sent to help them defend the Isthmus. But Themistocles was determined that his wooden wall would stay just where it was. When the war council met, he asked the other commanders to vote against the Spartan plan—but they were afraid. The Bay of Salamis was not a safe place, they said. It had only two little entrances, and the Persian fleet was already sitting just outside one of them. Themistocles answered that the two little entrances made the bay an ideal spot for a battle. If the Persians could be tempted into attacking, their ships would have to come into the bay one or two at a time. The Greek warships inside could easily pick them off.

While the council argued, Themistocles slipped out of the room and wrote a letter which he gave to a messenger to take secretly to Xerxes. In the letter he warned the Persian king that the Greek fleet was planning to leave the bay that night. He told Xerxes to block the entrances and to attack in the morning. He gave his promise that he and all the ships of Athens would desert the Greeks and fight for Persia.

Before evening, it was reported to the Greek war council that Xerxes had blocked off the other entrance to the bay. There could be no more talk of taking the fleet to the Isthmus. Instead, Themistocles outlined his plan for defeating the Persian attack.

Xerxes, too, sat in a council of war, but there were no arguments. When he ordered his admirals to sail into the bay at dawn, they looked at one another in surprise, but none of them dared to say that the plan was foolhardy. Then the king told them his secret—the battle was already as good as won, for Themistocles would fight on the Persian side. Xerxes ordered his golden throne set up on a platform on the shore, so that he would have a good view of the victory. While it was still dark, he had himself rowed to the beach and climbed onto the throne. At dawn, his ships began to move silently into the bay.

Themistocles' plan worked perfectly. The first Persian ships were sunk before they had a chance to fight. When more of them came into the bay, they jammed up until they could hardly move at all. They were easy targets for the Greeks, who nosed into them from the side, rowed hard, and smashed them into the shore.

Xerxes stood up on his throne and stamped his feet in rage. He howled orders across the water, cursing Themistocles and calling his admirals fools and cowards. By the end of the day more than two hundred of his ships had been sunk, while the others retreated and fled for the Hellespont. Xerxes went with them.

But more than a million enemy soldiers still occupied Greece. When Themistocles sent word of his sea victory to Sparta, he suggested that it was a good time for them to begin the fighting on land. The Spartans replied that they were eager

to do so, but unfortunately there had been an eclipse of the sun, a very bad omen. Winter came, and the Persian troops pulled back to their main camp in Thessaly. The Spartan generals waited at the Isthmus, and Themistocles tried to persuade them to do something about protecting Attica. In the spring, when the weather was good for fighting, the story was the same. By early summer, the Persians were moving south again, and the Spartans, though they said they wanted to help their Athenian friends, had a religious festival which kept them at home. Meanwhile, the Persian commander had sent an ambassador to Themistocles with an offer of peace on good terms. Themistocles' answer was short. "Tell your commander," he said to the ambassador, "that the Athenians say: 'So long as the sun rides through the sky, we will never come to terms with Xerxes.'" But when he wrote to the Spartans, he pretended that he had not yet made up his mind. He told them to move, and quickly, or he would accept the Persian offer. The Spartans decided that it was possible to march their troops north.

In August, the Greek army met the Persians near the little town of Plataea, about thirty miles from Athens. The Spartans had talked much and done little, but now that they were in battle, they lived up to their boasts. Even the Persian cavalry was no match against the superb Spartan foot soldiers. As the lines of Greek shields and spears moved relentlessly across the field, the horses bolted, and the lines of infantrymen scattered. Then the Persian commander was killed, and his soldiers dropped their shields and ran.

THE ASIANS LEAVE

There were no more battles. Dusty and tired, their armor tarnished and their food packs almost empty, the long columns of defeated Asians began the long march back to the Hellespont. They would not come again. Athenian ships and the soldiers of Sparta had saved Greece for the West.

For Themistocles, there was one more victory. When the generals and admirals went to their temples to thank the gods for helping them, they had to give special thanks for the men who had served Greece more worthily than all the others. Each of the commanders voted for himself as the most worthy and for Themistocles as the second most worthy. In a country where every man longs to be best, that was honor indeed.

THE BATTLE OF SALAMIS

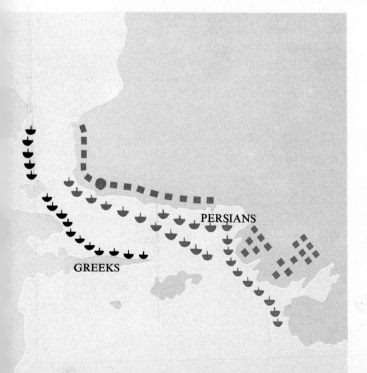

PERSIANS

GREEKS

The Golden Age of Athens

480 B.C.-430 B.C.

PERICLES

WHEN Themistocles and the people of Athens came home from Salamis, they found only the ashes of a city. Their houses and shops were gone. The Acropolis was littered with chunks of broken limestone and smoke-blackened statues, the ruins of their sacred temples. But the years of war had taught the Athenians courage, and victory gave them pride and hope. They began to build again.

While the citizens planned new houses, Themistocles planned new walls—walls around the city, walls to protect the harbor at Piraeus, and walls along the four miles of road that connected the two. When they were finished, Athens would be an island, surrounded by ramparts of stone instead of the sea, and as safe as Salamis.

The Spartans, already jealous of the Athenian navy, wanted badly to stop the work on the walls. They wrote to Themistocles and asked him to join them in a pact to outlaw all city walls in Greece. Themistocles knew well enough what they were after, but he agreed to go to Sparta to talk. Once he was there, he kept the talk going for weeks. When the Spartans heard that the walls were still going up, they complained. Themistocles suggested that they send ambassadors to Athens to look for themselves. When the ambassadors returned, they said that the walls were indeed being worked on. "No," Themistocles said, "by now they are finished." And he left the conference.

It was a Spartan sort of trick, and no one blamed Themistocles for it. In fact, many of the Greeks were pleased, not only because Sparta had been fooled, but because Athens was the city they looked to as their defender against the Persians.

The Spartans had lost interest in fighting Persians, once their own land was safe. Athens, however, had carried the fight across the ocean, freeing and protecting the Greek cities on the islands and in Asia Minor. Then Themistocles organized a league to defend Greece, and he offered the protection of the Athenian navy to everyone who joined. Dozens of cities, too small or too poor to pay for a strong fleet of their own, rushed to become members. Athens welcomed them all, and asked them only to give what they could to help the League—ships, if they had them, or contributions to the war treasury. The money was sent for safekeeping to the shrine of the Oracle on the sacred island of Delos, and people began to call the organization the Delian League.

THE ATHENIAN EMPIRE

Athens was, of course, much stronger than her allies. Some of the small cities began to wonder if "protecting" was the Athenian word for "ordering around." The Delian League was gradually turning into a private sea empire, bringing riches and power to the proud new city growing up around the Acropolis.

135

But there was no emperor in Athens. Themistocles was a general, a citizen whom other citizens had elected to do a job. To keep his job, he had to please the thousands of men who voted in the Assembly. They were still the real rulers of the *polis*.

When the Assembly met, on the wide, sloping plain below the hill called the Pnyx, the Herald cried: "Who wishes to speak?" Any citizen could answer, climb up the three stone steps to the platform, and have his say. But he had to speak well. The crowd was full of sharp-tongued fellows who liked nothing better than heckling a foolish speaker. They poked fun at his tangled words, confused his ideas, and finished him off with impolite comments on the shape of his nose or ears. Many young politicians gave up and hurried off the platform. But a man like Themistocles, one who chose his words well and sent them ringing across the hillside, could silence the wisecrackers in a minute. He could win elections too, and lead the people, not by commanding them, but by talking them into agreeing with his ideas.

It was impossible, however, to please all of the people all the time. The citizens were quick to forget a man's years of loyal service if he just once said or did something to displease them. The day came when Themistocles' speeches lost their magic. His enemies said he had become too proud, and the Athenians voted for him to leave the *polis*.

Their new favorite was Cimon, a big, jolly general whom no one could call too proud. He ate and drank with the people, joked with them, and tried to make them feel he was one of them. He had the walls of his garden torn down so that anyone could walk in and enjoy it. His table was always set with extra places for Athens' poor, and when he walked about the streets, he was followed by slaves who wore warm clothes and traded them for the tattered cloaks of penniless Athenians. But Cimon, too, was sent away. He and the citizens had agreed to be more friendly with Sparta. The Spartans answered with an insult, and the citizens of Athens changed their minds. Next, Cimon's chief rival was put out of the way, by murderers. That left Pericles as the leading citizen of Athens, and he was a very different sort of man from all the others.

Pericles was a nobleman. He was a quiet man, a scholar who had no patience for the whims by which many men ran their lives and cities. He rarely wandered among the common people, as Cimon had, and he refused to flatter them. Unlike Themistocles, he never hurried to speak in the Assembly. But when he did speak, he was called the "Zeus of Athens." It was said that he had thunder and lightning on his tongue. One man who tried to argue with him at the Assembly said that if he had wrestled Pericles and beaten him, Pericles could have persuaded the people who had watched that it had not happened.

There were politicians who said that, with such powers, Pericles could make himself the tyrant of Athens, or even its king. But Pericles was the grandnephew of Cleisthenes, the man who had started Athenian democracy. He said he would trust the votes of the citizens, and the citizens voted for him for more than thirty years. Pericles helped to make them years of greatness, a Golden Age of wealth and beauty and wisdom. All that was best in the Greek world came to Athens and seemed to become better there. Centuries later, when people spoke with wonder about "the glories of Greece," they usually meant Athens in the time of Pericles.

But Athens, the wonder of the world, was not a place where rich men built palaces, lived in luxury, and wore their gold around their necks and fingers and foreheads. The city streets were narrow and dark. The house fronts were plain, a stretch of unpainted clay brick wall with one door and no windows.

LIFE IN ATHENS

The house inside the wall was just as simple. The front door led to a courtyard, surrounded by columns and a covered porch, which was the sitting room in good weather. Doors from the porch led to a long dining room, a second courtyard for the women, the big room that belonged to the master and mistress of the house, and a row of dark little bedrooms and a tiny kitchen. There was no chimney for the kitchen fire, just a hole in the roof; when dinner was cooking, smoke often filled the room or blew out the door. The floors of the house were earth with a layer of pebbles beaten into it. Its furniture was well-made and handsome, but there was not much of it. There were couches in the dining room and bedrooms, a few low chairs and tables, footstools, and chests that served as cupboards.

When foreigners came to Athens, they were puzzled by these plain houses. Where, they asked, does Pericles live, and the people with money? "In houses like these," was the answer.

The Athenians, like most Greeks, had little interest in possessions, the comforts and luxuries that other people said they needed. The climate was so good that a man spent most of his time outdoors. His house was only a place for eating and sleeping. As for expensive clothes and fancy food, he had never had them, so he did not miss them, and he did not really want them.

When an Athenian gentleman woke up in the morning—on a couch that had neither springs nor sheets—he got up, folded a length of white wool cloth around him once, pinned it at the shoulders, tied on a sash, and he was dressed. If he was going out, as he always was, he would probably put on a cloak, too. He took a minute or two to set the folds just so; people judged a man by the careful arrangement of his clothes. His breakfast was a cup of wine mixed with honey and hot water—morning coffee in Athens —and a toasted barley cake. He did not use butter, because butter was an ointment for rubbing into the skin. He had heard that the people in Thebes ate the stuff, but it sounded like a disgusting habit, and no Athenian would try it.

After breakfast, he set out for the market place. His first stop was the barber shop, where he had his beard trimmed and his hair combed. Here, too, he caught up on the news. Athens had no newspapers, but the barber shop served the purpose very well. Next he went to buy groceries at the stalls under the awnings on the north side of the square. He sent his slave home with the food, and then it was time for business.

Merchants and craftsmen kept shop in the side streets or in the *stoas*, the long covered porches that overlooked the square. Bankers and shipping men also met their clients in the *stoas*. In fact, nearly everyone took a stroll through the porches at some time during the morning, because there was always someone there to talk to. Talk was Athens' favorite occupation.

The morning's business was often government business. Pericles said that a man who took no part in his city's democracy was worse than harmless, he was useless. When the Assembly met, once every ten days or so, a rope dripping with red paint was swept across the market place to hurry up the dawdlers, and a red blot on a man's cloak cost him a fine. But voting was only one part of a citizen's duties. All the day-to-day jobs of running the *polis* were done by citizens. They

served for a year, then handed over their duties to other citizens. Well-known men were elected to the important councils, but anyone might be chosen as a juryman, an official of his clan, a market inspector, or a record keeper. Pericles had arranged for small salaries to be paid for many of the jobs so that poor men would not be made poorer by working for the city. A citizen, however, would often work without pay.

TIME FOR LEISURE

Time was the one thing in which a Greek was rich—time for his *polis*, time for the talk he loved, time to enjoy himself. Slaves did some of his work. Foreign craftsmen, who were not citizens, made many of the things he used, and foreign merchants ran the shops where he bought them. His wife and the household slaves took care of his home. And since he had no use for many of the things people of other countries said they needed, he did not have to spend his time

GREEK KNIGHTS, AS SHOWN ON THE
FRIEZE OF THE PARTHENON

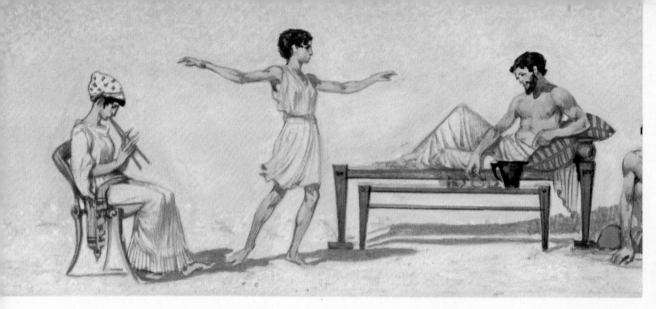

AT BANQUETS, ATHENIANS WERE ENTERTAINED BY SINGERS, DANCERS, AND MUSICIANS.

earning the money to buy them. When he went for lunch—an egg or some fish, with fruit for dessert—his day's business was usually finished.

After lunch, he went back to the market place for a chat or walked out to the Lyceum or the Academy, the athletic fields in the lovely open country outside the city walls. There he and his friends strolled along the paths that wound through the olive groves at the edges of the fields—or perhaps they found seats on the benches and watched the young men practicing for the Games. Some of them left the loungers and ran out to exercise with the athletes, wrestling, running, or hurling javelins. From time to time, the young men came in from the field to join one of the gatherings in the grove. Some of the groups were like clubs; the same men met together every day. Others gathered around one man, a teacher or wise man who had come to Athens because it was a place where he was free to speak his mind.

When the shadows of the olive trees, lengthening along the ground, showed that sunset was only an hour or two away, the strollers started to the city to get ready for dinner. If they were invited out, they stopped first at the public bath. There a slave rubbed them with the olive oil which did for soap, then scraped off the oil and the dirt with a metal scraper, and finished the "bath" with a dousing of cold water from a pitcher. It was said that some people had taken to bathing in tubs of warm water, but, like eating butter, it was something an Athenian did not care to try.

At dusk, the guests knocked on their host's front door. All of them were men, for no respectable lady dined in the company of any man except her husband. As the guests came into the house, they kicked off their sandals. A slave washed the street dust from their feet. He gave them garlands of flowers to wear, and showed them into the dining room. There the fine wooden couches, with their inlay of ivory and silver or gold, had been brushed. Small tables were drawn up to them, and oil lamps threw a soft light. The guests lay on the couches, propped up by pillows and their left elbows. They were light eaters, not like the old Achaeans. They enjoyed a bit of sausage, meat pudding, and roasted pigeon. They liked the flavors to be strong, and their favorite vegetable was garlic. Since they had only one hand free to pick up food, the dinner was cut up by servants before it was brought to the tables. There were no knives and forks, and spoons were used only for soft things, like eggs. Otherwise the diners ate with their fingers, wiping them on napkins or bits of bread.

EVENING IN ATHENS

When the guests had had their fill, the slaves took away the tables and brought them back with dessert—fruit, cakes, nuts, and olives. Then, with much ceremony, the wine was served. It was rich and thick as syrup, so it usually was mixed with water. The slaves did the mixing in a huge bowl, then ladled the wine into wide, shallow cups made of pottery as thin and delicate as fine china.

THE *SYMPOSIUM*

The evening's entertainment, the *Symposium*, began. First, the host poured out three cups of wine as sacrifices to the Gods of Olympus, to the Heroes, and to Zeus. He wished his guests good health, and they toasted him in return. Then he called for the entertainers—slave girls who danced and played flutes, or a singer who accompanied himself on a lyre. At a big party, there might also be clowns or acrobats or jugglers. But the Athenians were well prepared to entertain themselves. Each man had his own stock of songs to sing. And always there was talk. At some houses, it was jokes and riddles; at others, it was a serious discussion of Athens' problems and the chances of war, or an argument about the life of man or the ways of the gods. What other men did in books, the Greeks did in talk.

When the lamps flickered low and the men began to nod, a final cup of wine was sacrificed to Hermes, the messenger god who guarded travelers on the road. The guests wished their host good night. Outside in the street, their slaves waited with torches to light the way home. Around the corner came the young guests from another party, marching six abreast and singing at the top of their voices. And when the first cocks crowed in the morning, it was time again to go to the market place.

It was a good life, and if a man's house was plain, he had only to look at the Acropolis to see the most beautiful buildings in the world. The smoke-stained ruins were gone, dragged off the Rock by the order of Pericles. Now he and the Athenians were covering the hill with splendid new temples for the gods who had helped them to defeat the Persians.

Pericles had hired the finest architects in Greece. He had asked a friend, the great sculptor Phidias, to plan the carvings and the statues. When the work started, nearly every artist and craftsman in Athens had a part in it. It was not a job for gangs of slaves, like those who had built the Egyptians' temples. In fact, there were no great gangs of workmen at all. Each craftsman made a contract to do a small portion of the work. A stonecutter was hired to shape one column. A man with a cart agreed to haul so many pieces of marble. He did the job with his own little crew of several freemen and slaves. As the columns grew tall, carpenters were hired to build the wooden roofs, and Phidias' sculptors began to carve the rows of figures on the marble slabs that ran along the tops of the columns. In other parts of the city, foundrymen were already casting the great bronze statues. Goldsmiths, dyers, tapestry weavers, and workers in ivory were fashioning thousands of decorations for the gods' new homes.

Each man tried to outdo all the others, to make his work the most perfect piece of work. Phidias himself made the colossal bronze statue of Athena of the Vanguard, which was to go near the entrance of the Acropolis. For Athena's temple, he carved another statue of the goddess, this one of ivory. She seemed to have a skin that glowed with life, and her golden cloak hung so softly that it seemed to move in the breeze.

In the old days, the Greeks' statues had not looked half so real. The handsome stone figures had strength, but they were stiff. Then sculptors

SCULPTORS AT WORK

like Phidias came to understand more about anatomy, the way bones link together and muscles change shape when men move. Their new statues were graceful and true to life. When people saw them, they thought of the tale of Pygmalion, the sculptor who fell in love with his own statue of a woman and begged Aphrodite to bring her to life so he could marry her. But Pygmalion's statue, like all the rest, was more beautiful than any real

ICTINUS, THE ARCHITECT OF THE PARTHENON, DISCUSSING HIS PLAN WITH PERICLES

person. A Greek was not satisfied with things as they were. When he made something, he tried to make it perfect. It was his way to be a little like a god. The architect who planned a temple tried to find the one shape that was so right that no change could possibly make it better.

As the work on the Acropolis went on, watching the builders became the favorite pastime in Athens. A crew with a tricky job to do was sure to have a good-sized audience. Pericles himself kept a sharp eye on the project, and he was pleased to see how quickly it was going. Soon the stonecutters and carpenters had finished, and painters climbed the scaffolding to add touches of purple, blue, and crimson to the white of the marble. The statues were then set into place.

Then the world came to see Athens' Acropolis, for the stories of its magnificent beauty had already spread across the Mediterranean. As travelers sailed into the port at Piraeus, they could see the gleam of bronze from the spear of Phidias' giant Athena on the mountain four miles away. When they reached the city and walked up the Acropolis itself, they passed first through a vast entryway with five tall doorways and rows of columns topped with a brightly painted ceiling. This was the *Propylea,* the gates of the sacred hill. To the left, the visitors saw a gallery of pictures. On the right, perched high upon a rock, was the beautiful little temple that belonged to Nike, the goddess of victory. Beyond the doorways were the halls where pilgrims gathered, but most visitors walked on, into the brilliant sunlight of the hilltop. Before them, towering five stories high, stood the bronze goddess whose spear they had seen from the harbor. The Erectheum, a temple built to honor a founder of the city, was on their left. But when they could take their eyes off the goddess, they looked first to the right, for there stood the greatest of Greek temples.

THE PARTHENON

The Parthenon, Athena's own house, was built of creamy white marble from the slopes of Mount Pontelicus in Attica. In time—a thousand years or more—the iron that was in the stone turned it a soft honey color. But nothing could change the fact that Ictinus, the architect whom Pericles asked to plan the temple, had found that one perfect design for which he searched. To the visitors who stared up at his great building, it

ATHENIANS, SUCH AS THE SOLDIER AT LEFT, OFTEN STOPPED TO OBSERVE THE CON-STRUCTION OF THE PARTHENON.

somehow gave the feeling of both calm and power, just as Athena was the goddess of both wisdom and war. Ictinus had been afraid that a building so big would seem to sit heavily on the earth, so he planned the platform on which it stood to curve upward at the center. He had noticed, too, that when he stood near tall buildings, the walls seemed to lean out, even though they were really straight. To overcome this, he made the columns thicker at the middle and tilted them slightly inward.

Phidias and his sculptors had given their finest work to the Parthenon. At each end, in the triangular spaces under the roof, their carvings showed important events in the life of Athena; her birth and her contest with the god Poseidon for the honor of Athens. The great procession of the Panathenaic Festival paraded around the topmost walls of the temple in a long sculpture inside the row of columns. On the outside of the long pieces of stone that ran across the tops of the columns, marble gods fought fierce marble giants, and the old tribe of Lapiths battled galloping Centaurs carved in stone. Each sculpture taught a lesson as well as told a tale. To the Greeks, the victory of the gods and the Lapiths showed the victory of order over the unruly strength of beasts. It was the wisdom of Athens that had turned barbarians into the men of a Golden Age.

The Acropolis was dedicated to Athena. Honored with the most perfect beauty that the minds and hands of men could make, she stood above her city, the city of war and wisdom.

Greek Against Greek

430 B.C.-404 B.C.

ABOUT 425 B.C., a lonely man, in a country that was not his own, sat down to write the story of a war that had begun six years before. Thucydides, an Athenian, had fought in the war's first battles. He had been a general, in command of thousands of his city's troops. Then he was ordered to go to the aid of another commander whose men were outnumbered. When he arrived, the battle had already been fought and lost. It was not his fault. But the people of Athens were too anxious about the war to consider that. They stripped Thucydides of his command and forced him to leave his homeland. Now, while the war raged on, he could only watch, and he was troubled by the things he saw.

Athens and its old rival Sparta were caught in a deadly struggle to see which would be the master of the Greek world. Men died, cities were destroyed, and nothing was gained, but the war went on. Thucydides began to write about the senseless fighting, hoping that he might teach the men of another time to avoid war. He wrote of the ambassadors from the city of Corinth, who spoke to the Spartans in their assembly, warning them about Athens.

"You have no idea what kind of people these

Athenians are," the Corinthians said, "how altogether different from you. They are always thinking up new schemes, and they are quick to make plans and to do something about them. But you are happy with what you have and slow to do even what is necessary. The Athenians are bold and adventurous; you Spartans are cautious and afraid to trust your own strength. They love foreign adventure, which you hate, because they think there is something to win, while you think that something might be lost. . . . When they make a plan, and it fails, they are sorry. But if it succeeds, they say it's nothing compared to what they are going to do next. It is simply impossible for them to enjoy peace and quiet themselves or to allow anyone else to do so."

The Corinthians themselves were worried about losing their rich trading routes to the western Mediterranean. Athenian traders were looking greedily in that direction. Athens had just decided to send military aid to Corcyra, a colony that was trying to break away from the Corinthians, who had founded it. Corinth had signed a pact with Sparta; when either city went to war, so must the other. Now the Corinthians demanded that the Spartans lead the attack against Athens, and they agreed.

Thucydides said that Corinth's quarrel with Athens was only the excuse for the war; it was not the reason for it. The true reason, he said, was power. Sparta's power came from its army, which was the strongest in the world. The king of Persia still dreamed of owning Greece, and he hoped to make his dreams come true by encouraging Athens and Sparta to destroy each other. He was sure that the two rival cities would not long be satisfied with sharing the Greek world. Sooner or later, one would try to make use of its power to conquer the other. And that was what happened, for with power came greed.

Sparta had always been strong and selfish, but Athens was just as strong. The Athenians had begun to enjoy spending the money that came from their island allies, and they wanted more. The *polis* that was democratic at home became a tyrant on the seas, gobbling up smaller cities. Sparta, fearing for its own empire in the Peloponnesus, started to collect cities, too. The Greek world began to seem too small for the greedy

ATHENIAN SOLDIERS GOING INTO BATTLE
AGAINST SPARTA

rivals to share it. They held a peace conference, agreed not to fight, and went on drilling their troops. Then Corinth gave Sparta a push, and in 431 B.C., the Peloponnesian War began.

Spartan troops marched into Attica. Pericles called for the people of the countryside to come into the city, the "island" inside Themistocles' walls. When they gathered in the market place, clutching their bundles of clothes and pots and tools, Pericles spoke to them. It was useless, he said, to waste Athenian lives in a fight to save Attica; Sparta's army was too strong. But the Spartans could do nothing against Athens' ships, and Sparta was poor, while Athens was rich. Safe inside the city walls, with the fleet to bring them food, the people of Athens had only to wait until the Spartans ran out of money and went home.

The country people nodded silently. Then they picked up their bundles and went to find places to stay in the city. Some found room in the temples and government offices. The rest set up tents and makeshift huts between the long walls that ran from Athens to the harbor at Piraeus. There they stayed for weeks, and then months. In the winter, the Spartan soldiers went home. But they came back in the spring, tramping across the fields of Attica, setting fire to the groves and pulling down the houses.

PLAGUE IN ATHENS

Then the city was invaded by an enemy more deadly than the Spartans. A sailor, just returned from a foreign port, fell sick and died. Soon after, several people in Piraeus came down with the same sickness, and they died, too. The doctors were puzzled. But when people in the huts between the Long Walls began to die in the same strange way, they became frightened. The sickness was the plague. There was no cure for it, and no way to stop it from spreading through the crowded city.

In a year, it killed more than a third of Athens' people. Weakened by illness, weary from long months of guard duty along the walls, the Athenians turned on Pericles in anger. His plan had brought them nothing but losses and death, they said. Pericles called a meeting of the Assembly. When the Herald cried, "Who would speak?" he answered, as he had so many times before, "I, Pericles." But when he climbed to the stone platform, there was no cheer. The men on

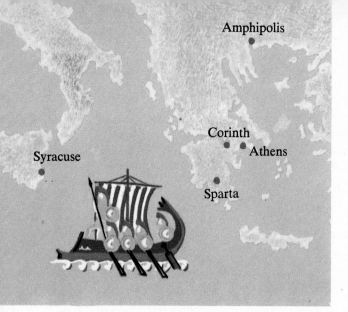

MAP SHOWS LOCATION OF GREEK CITIES

the hillside were thin and hollow-eyed, and they did not trust him. He began to speak. He reminded the citizens that he had brought them the riches of an empire, and that they had voted with him to fight Sparta. There was a rumble of disagreement from the crowd.

"I have not changed," Pericles said, "but *you* have changed. You will not stand by the plans you voted for when everything was going well. You can not blame me for that."

The people would not listen. They voted Pericles out of office and fined him for doing his job badly. A few weeks later, they apologized and elected him again, because Athens could not get along without him. But he had changed. His handsome face was marked by lines of worry, and he seemed tired. Then he fell ill and died, killed by the plague that had killed so many of his people.

In his book, Thucydides told how the citizens of Athens lost their good sense when they lost Pericles. While the Spartans plodded along, getting on with the job and never altering their plans or questioning their generals, the Athenians changed their minds time and again. They voted for one man as long as he won battles; when he lost a fight, they looked for someone else. Each time they were sure that they had found a new Pericles, a "man of the hour" who would lead them to victory and riches, or at least to peace. Thucydides knew the story well; he was one of the men they had sent away. Others managed to stay.

There was Nicias, an aristocrat and a general.

He was a cautious man who took great care to find out the will of the gods before he did anything. It was said that he kept a fortuneteller in his house, to tell him what was best for Athens, and how to invest his money for the greatest profit. When Nicias led an army, he did what was safe. If he never did anything adventurous, the people could be sure, at least, that he had never done anything wrong. Nicias was for peace.

On the other side were the new politicians, common men who were making names for themselves by speaking well, or loudly, at the Assembly: Cleon, the leather merchant; Eucrates, the rope seller; and Hyperbolus, the lamp maker. They were impatient men, anxious for Athens to fight instead of waiting.

Cleon called himself "the People's watchdog." The citizens said it was because at every meeting of the Assembly he barked at the heels of Nicias and the generals. One morning, the generals explained their reasons for not attacking a Spartan army which the fleet had cornered on an island. Cleon asked to speak, as usual. As he climbed heavily to the platform, the people nudged each other; Cleon was in his bulldog mood. He began by sneering at the generals. Then he told them that, if they had any courage at all, they could easily take the trapped Spartans. "Why, if I were a general," he said, "I'd capture them myself."

Nicias stepped forward and quietly offered to lend him the troops to do it. Cleon thought it was a bluff. He told Nicias that he was ready to go whenever the generals gave the word. Then he saw that Nicias meant what he said, and he tried to back out. But the crowd, already chuckling, had heard enough of his boasts. The more he tried to refuse the command, the more they shouted for him to take it and sail. At last, when he saw that there was no way out, Cleon accepted. He boasted that within twenty days he would bring back the Spartans—unless, of course, he killed them on the spot. The Athenians roared, and even the most serious men at the Assembly smiled. So far as they could see, only two things could happen. Either they would be rid of Cleon, which was just as well, or the Spartan outpost would be defeated.

To everyone's amazement, Cleon came home victorious, and his prisoners included Spartan officers. He was elected a general and went off on new campaigns. Meanwhile, cautious Nicias was trying to end the war. Battles were all very well, if one won them, he said. But if one lost—well, that was a different story.

In 423 B.C., a committee of Spartans came to Nicias to talk about a truce. But Cleon persuaded the Assembly to give him an army, and he marched north to chase the Spartans. At Amphipolis, a town in Thrace, he ran into an enemy army commanded by Brasidas, a Spartan who had as little use for the peacemakers as Cleon did. When Cleon saw his fierce opponent, he did not want to fight, but the Spartans charged. Brasidas proved to have more bravery than sense: he led the first wave of men and was killed. Cleon, too, died while leading his troops in a dash for safety.

THE PEACE OF NICIAS

After that, the Athenians were willing to listen when Nicias talked about a truce. In 421 B.C., the representatives of the two cities signed a treaty, the "Peace of Nicias." It called for fifty years of peace, and it left things almost exactly as they had been before the ten years of war. When the terms were announced, Sparta's allies were furious. The Corinthians immediately went off to find other cities that might be willing to fight the Athenians for them. And in Athens, the citizens, as usual, began to change their minds.

Nicias now had a new rival in the Assembly, a handsome young nobleman whose name was Alcibiades. He was a kinsman of Pericles, but he was as lighthearted and reckless as Pericles had been thoughtful. In battle, where other men wore armor decorated with the stern emblems of war, Alcibiades carried a gold-plated shield with a picture of Cupid tossing a thunderbolt. In the city, he trailed through the market place in an elegant purple robe. He was the last man to leave a party, and the first to begin singing on the way home. But when he spoke in the Assembly, the people listened, for he was a clever speaker. Nicias, with his talk of peace, seemed dull beside him.

Alcibiades was for action. He urged the Athenians to think again before they gave up the wealth which their power could bring them. He told them about the island of Sicily and its great city, Syracuse. He talked of a new empire of Athens that would spread from Sicily across the western sea, to Africa and Spain, as far as the Pillars of Hercules. He talked of adventure and countless ships and gold.

As the Athenians listened to Alcibiades, they forgot that Athens had once stood for freedom against a foreign tyrant. They forgot, too, that

Sicily was far away and so big that it took a ship eight days to sail around it. They did not think about the defenses which a great city like Syracuse was certain to have. They remembered Marathon and Salamis, and forgot that then they had fought for their homeland on a battlefield and a bay which they knew as well as they knew the streets of Athens.

No one in the city thought of anything but Sicily. At the Lyceum and the Academy, groups of young men plotted out campaigns on maps of the island which they sketched on the ground. Their fathers met in the market place and considered the costs, comparing them to the treasure that would come back when the battles had been won. In the government offices, the lists of ships and rowers were drawn up.

When the Assembly met, Nicias spoke once more for peace. "Is it really a good thing," he asked, "to send the ships at all? When you go to Sicily, you leave many enemies behind you and make new ones there." He called for the older, wiser men of Athens to vote against Alcibiades. He was too young to command such a great expedition, Nicias said, and he wanted the campaign only to win himself a name. Then Nicias reminded the citizens that Alcibiades was so eager for fame that he had once entered seven chariots in the Olympic Games, all drawn by his own expensive horses. How far could a man go to glorify himself?

Alcibiades did not apologize for his pride. He said: "I have a better right than others to hold the command, and I think that I am worthy." As for the seven chariots, he had raced them for the glory of Athens, and he had won first, second, and fourth places. The war in Sicily would be for Athens' glory, too. "We may rule the whole of Greece," he shouted, "and certainly we will humble the Syracusans."

The Assembly cheered and voted to send the expedition. Then they named three men to command it: Alcibiades, of course; Lamachus, a skillful general; and Nicias, who did not want to go. On a bright morning, early in the summer of 415 B.C., the people of Athens flocked to the docks at Piraeus to watch the expedition leave. They cheered as the soldiers, 30,000 strong, climbed aboard their ships. No one went home until the last vessel had moved across the water and set its course for Syracuse.

Before the week was out, the Athenians were changing their minds again. Now that Alcibiades was gone, his enemies, the politicians who hated him for his riches and his way with the people, could speak freely. They accused him of insulting the gods, and said that he was to blame for the gang of ruffians who had smashed many of Athens' sacred statues one night before the expedition sailed. If Alcibiades commanded the expedition, the politicians warned, the gods would strike him down, and all the soldiers with him.

Alcibiades' friends replied that Corinthian spies had destroyed the statues in order to frighten the men who were leaving for Sicily. But the citizens, afraid of angering the gods, refused to listen to reason. Though Alcibiades had planned the whole Syracuse campaign, they took his command away from him. A messenger was sent to tell him to come home to stand trial for insulting the gods.

Alcibiades did not come back. Instead, he fled to the Peloponnesus, and then to Sparta. He was too proud to stand aside, like Thucydides, while the war went on without him. If Athens would not have him, he would fight for Athens' enemies. He became an adviser to the Spartan kings and began to plan the defeat of the armies he had once commanded.

Meanwhile, Nicias and Lamachus had led the Athenian expedition to Sicily. They won few victories, for the Sicilians were hard fighters and the strange battlefields were full of traps. Even so, the Athenians pushed on toward Syracuse. Then Lamachus was killed, leaving only Nicias to lead the attack on the biggest city in the Greek world. He was the wrong man for the job. Cautious as ever, he was slow to attack, afraid to take risks, and never sure of himself or his men. The expedition came to a halt outside the walls of Syracuse, and there it sat. Reinforcements arrived from Athens, but still Nicias waited, while the Syracusans strengthened their defenses and persuaded Sparta to come to their aid.

When the Spartans landed on Sicily, Nicias decided to retreat. It would be no victory, but at least he could get his men on the ships and run for the open sea before the harbor at Syracuse was blocked. But on the night that the ships were to sail, there was an eclipse of the moon. Nicias was certain that it was a bad omen. His fortune-teller agreed and advised him to wait for a full moon.

While Nicias waited, the enemy navy sailed across the harbor, attacked, and defeated the great fleet from Athens. The Athenians beached their ships or left them to sink, and tried to escape by land. For days the worn-out army plodded on, without food or water. The rear half fell behind and was easily captured. Then the Syracusans moved in to finish off the rest. The last troop of Athenians was caught on the bank of a river. They were so thirsty that they did not care when the enemy soldiers came at them. They ran for the water and drank it as they died.

Seven thousand Athenians, all that were left of the great expedition, were thrown into the Syracusan stone quarries. There, with no shelter from the summer's burning sun or the bitter cold of winter, they grew weak and all but a few died. Those who lived owed their lives to poetry. When gentlemen sightseers came out from Syracuse to have a look at the quarries, they heard some of the captives chanting the lines of plays which they had seen in Athens. The Syracusans stared. Then, realizing that these bony men in rags had once been gentlemen, too, they pitied them. They arranged to buy their freedom, in return for more speeches from the plays.

When the citizens of Athens heard the stories of those few half-dead men who came back from Syracuse, they at first refused to believe them. When they did, they forgot that they had voted for Alcibiades themselves, and remembered only the men—and the treasure—which they had lost. They clamored for new generals, and new fleets—and victories. Gold and silver decorations were stripped from the Acropolis and melted down to pay for more ships. Slaves were offered their freedom if they fought for Athens. But there was no talk of ending the war.

ATHENS DEFEATED

The Spartans, too, were eager to fight again, for now they had a fleet as well as an army. The ships were a gift from the king of Persia, who had decided that it was time for him to lend a hand in the war that was destroying Greece. When the Spartans marched into Attica again, the new battleships sailed into the Aegean. They attacked the merchant vessels which took supplies to Athens and cruised around the island allies, encouraging them to desert the Delian League. The king of Persia did not say what he meant to do when the island had been "set free" from Athens' protection, but he was greatly pleased with the success of the Spartan cruises.

Panic swept Athens. Thucydides called it a kind

of madness, the last symptoms of the greed which had so changed the city. Athenian justice was forgotten. The island allies were taxed until they had no money left. When one of the little cities begged to stay out of the war, Athens sent the fleet with orders to execute all the men in the city and to sell their families into slavery. This was not cruelty, the Athenians said; it was showing the world that Athens was still powerful.

The citizens began to distrust each other. Leaders elected one day were executed the next. A group of commanders who came home with news of a victory at sea were arrested for losing too many men in the battle. Hauled before the Assembly, the commanders were condemned to death by the democracy which they had defended. For a few months, democracy itself was forgotten, while a Council of 400 ruled Athens. But the Assembly soon took over again, shouting and wrangling.

One summer evening in 405 B.C., the ship *Paralus* docked at Piraeus. One of the sailors stopped at a barber shop before going into the city. A minute or two later, another man dashed out of the shop, howling, his face wet with tears. As he ran toward Athens, a chorus of wailing followed him along the Long Walls, and then shouts and sobbing filled the city. The news which the sailor had brought to the gossips in the barber shop was the worst that Athens could hear. At Aegospotami on the Hellespont, a squadron of Spartan warships had utterly defeated the Athenian fleet.

Athens held out for a year. Men, allies, ships, money—all were gone. Enemy troops camped outside the city walls and enemy ships blocked the harbor at Piraeus, waiting for the Athenians to starve or surrender. Thucydides received a message from the Assembly, a polite invitation to return to Athens. There was nothing he could do to help the city now, but he went, because Athens was his home. He was there when the people begged for Sparta's terms and the Athenian leaders signed the agreement.

Peace came in the summer of 404 B.C., after twenty-seven years of war. The Spartan flutes struck up a tune. Soldiers, decked with garlands, began to throw down the stones of Themistocles' great walls. Athens had been forced to agree to that, and to give up its league of cities and all but twelve of its warships. But the city was not destroyed, and its people were not sold as slaves. Thucydides was grateful. They were better terms than the Athenians might have given the Spartans, if the war had gone the other way.

MORE THAN 20,000 ATHENIANS WERE KILLED NEAR THE CITY OF SYRACUSE IN SICILY.

The Greek Way of Life

700 B.C. - 343 B.C.

IN THE first years of Spartan peace, Greece was filled with wandering soldiers. Their little cities needed them no more. The new governments, which the Spartans appointed, looked on them as men who might make trouble, and were quick to get rid of them. Homeless, and with no way to earn a living, the old campaigners roamed from place to place. They became soldiers of fortune, men who fought for any general or city that offered pay and three meals a day. In 401 B.C., ten thousand of them hired themselves out to Cyrus, a prince of Persia, who hoped to steal his brother's throne.

The Army of Ten Thousand was an odd lot. There were officers and men from a dozen or more Greek states, soldiers who had fought with and against each other during the thirty years of war that had torn Greece apart. Yet, under a foreign commander, they worked together well. They made a strong force which no Asian army could begin to match. Cyrus led them far into Persia, and wherever they went they were victorious. Then Cyrus was killed in battle and the Greek officers were tricked and treacherously murdered. The great army suddenly found itself stranded, with neither money nor leaders. The men were not even sure where they were, except that it was hundreds of miles from the coast and Greece.

ELECTION OF XENOPHON

The Persian king waited for them to lose heart and surrender, as any Asian army did when it had no officers to give it orders. But the Army of Ten Thousand was Greek. After a day of confusion, the soldiers called an Assembly and elected a new general, Xenophon, a young Athenian who had been the assistant of one of the dead officers. For four months he led them through a wilderness of mountains, while Persian cavalrymen harried them and icy winds cut through their flimsy summer uniforms. Their food was whatever they could take from the strongholds of mountain tribes along the way. Gradually, they abandoned their baggage and the prizes they had won in battle; it took all their strength simply to go on.

One day, as the weary army dragged itself to

THIS STATUE OF THE 5TH CENTURY B.C. SHOWS ZEUS CARRYING GANYMEDE OFF TO OLYMPUS TO BE HIS CUPBEARER.

the top of another steep hill, the men in the lead gave a great shout. Xenophon, thinking it was an ambush, rushed to the front of the column, but he found no fighting and his soldiers standing with tears running down their faces. They pointed ahead, beyond the slope of the mountain and the fields below. "The sea," they shouted, "the sea!"

To a Greek, the sea meant home. The long march was over.

When his men had returned safely to Greece, Xenophon gave up his command, but he did not go home. Athens had sent him away, and the citizens did not invite him to return. The Spartans, however, offered him an estate in the Peloponnesus, a fine piece of land with a wide meadow, a stream, and thickly wooded hills. Xenophon loved hunting and fishing, and he accepted the Spartan offer. He built a house especially designed to catch the sunlight all the year, planted an orchard with every sort of fruit tree known in Greece, and settled down, content. In the mornings, while the mists still drifted across his meadow, he and his hounds chased wild boar and deer. After lunch, he worked at a book he was writing.

Like Thucydides, Xenophon was an exile, far from his home. Like him, he had lived through the dreadful time when Athens tried to win the world and lost everything. But his book was not a tragic tale of men and cities ruined by war. Thucydides had told only one part of the story of the Greeks. Xenophon told another. He wrote about the bravery of the Ten Thousand, about good fellows who dined together and talked until dawn, and about the best of times in a splendid world of Greeks. That was the world which he and his soldiers had feared they might never see again. It was a pleasant book about a pleasant life, a little stuffy sometimes and old-fashioned, like Xenophon himself.

Other men told other parts of the story. They remembered the days before the war, and the months when the fighting had been far from the city. Then Pericles' Golden Age continued, they said. Life was good, and Greece was still a land of poets, athletes, and wise men. Later, when people who were not Greeks read the books, they were sometimes confused. It did not seem possible that all the writers were talking about the same place. The readers had forgotten that one Greek could be many things—a soldier one day, a merchant the next, and a statesman the day after that.

Xenophon, the young adventurer, became a country squire. He puttered about his orchard and

ATHLETES TRAINED HARD FOR THE OLYMPIC GAMES,
WHICH INCLUDED TRACK AND FIELD EVENTS.

entertained the friends who came for a week or two of quiet. Once every four years, however, his house overflowed with guests. Athenian friends and old companions from the long march turned up from every part of Greece to attend the games at Olympia, just two and a half miles down the road. They stabled their horses in the meadow, set up camp in the orchard, and each morning they rode out to watch the contests.

At Olympia, a city of tents had sprung up around the temples and the stadium. Every *polis* put up a camp for its own athletes and trainers. There were dining pavilions, gymnasiums, and a long row of peddlers' booths, like the midway at a fair. There were beggars, fortunetellers, and souvenir-sellers, and even scholars who showed

off their skills to the thousands who had come to see the games.

No quarrel between men or cities was allowed to interfere with the great festival. A month-long truce protected the athletes who had to travel through enemy territory on their way to Olympia. No city dared to break that truce, for the Olympic Games were sacred.

THE FIRST OLYMPIC GAMES

At Olympia, it was said, Zeus had fought with his father Cronus for the right to rule the universe. To celebrate his victory, he called for the gods to match their strength and skill on the same

150

CONTESTANTS HAD TO TAKE AN OATH THAT THEY
HAD BEEN IN TRAINING FOR TEN MONTHS.

field. In those first Olympic Games, Apollo out-raced Hermes, the wing-footed messenger of the gods. He boxed with Ares, the god of war, and defeated him.

Later, when the greatest athletes of Greece came to Olympia with dreams of winning victories like Apollo's, Zeus was still the guardian and final judge of the contests. His statue, a huge figure of gold and ivory, stood above the fields. On the first day of the festival the athletes brought their sacrifices to his altar. They prayed for victory, and swore to compete fairly.

Then came the four days of contests. First there were junior events, for lads eighteen and younger —sprints, track events, and wrestling. The men's contests began on the third day of the festival.

There were footraces, including a 200-yard dash and an endurance run of two or three miles. Then the heavyweights took over the field for *Pancration*, a rugged hand-to-hand fight for two men, which combined boxing and wrestling. In practice, the athletes wore caps to protect their heads and ears, but at Olympia they fought without them. They hammered at each other with fists bound with leather strips, which saved their knuckles but did nothing to soften their blows. They tried to throw each other with a "flying mare" or a "wrestlers' heave." Anything was allowed, except biting and eye-gouging, and the fight continued until one of the contenders gave the sign of defeat. Sometimes the battle was ended by death.

151

The fourth day brought the *Pentathlon,* a less savage contest for all-around athletes. Each man had to compete in the five events: sprinting, regular wrestling, the discus throw, the javelin toss, and the long jump. The discus was a round, plate-like weight of stone or metal, thrown for distance. The spearlike javelin was thrown for accuracy at a target. In the long jump, an odd sort of broad jump, the athletes were not allowed a running start; instead, they held heavy weights which they tossed behind them when they leaped, to give themselves an extra push forward.

While these events were going on in the Stadium, there were others in the Hippodrome, the horse arena. There, bareback riders raced their mounts, and charioteers, some of them kings or princes, showed off the fastest teams in Greece. The chariot racing was wild. The drivers urged on their horses, tilted and crashed against other chariots, risking anything to come in first.

Winning was the aim of every man at the Games. In other times and places, athletes found a kind of reward in playing a game well, whether they won or lost. But for a Greek, victory was the only thing that mattered. He spent years training himself, then tried his strength in the games in his own city. If he won these home-town meets, he went on to Olympia and the three other international contests: the Isthmian Games at Corinth, the Pythian Games at Delphi, and the Nemean Games which, like the Olympics, were held in the Peloponnesus. At each of them he tried to prove that he was the best man, and to show the gods that he had the strongest will to win.

THE LAURELS

The winners' prizes at Olympia, awarded at the ceremony on the last day of the festival, were simple wreaths of olive leaves. But it meant fame and honor which only the greatest heroes could expect. As the victor rode home, he was hailed in town after town. The important men of his own *polis* came to meet him on the road and formed a procession to conduct him into the city. Sometimes a section of the city wall was torn down, making a new gateway for the victor. "What need have we for walls," the people said, "with such men to defend us?" They put him into a four-horse chariot and led him to the shrine of the city's guardian god. There he placed his wreath on the altar as an offering. A feast was given in his

honor, and when the banqueting was over and the toasts drunk, there was singing by the chorus that performed at all the city's festivals. This night they chanted a new ode, a song which told of the athlete's victory.

No one thought it odd that a serious poem should be written about a foot race or a wrestling match. Pindar, the greatest writer of odes, wrote his poems in praise of athletes. A victor, he thought, had something of a god in him, and the new heroes of the Games were a sign that Greece still had men like Homer's heroes. A poem was a proper way to tell about such godlike men, or about anything so important that it ought to be remembered.

Whenever a Greek read Homer's poems, the Achaeans seemed to live again. Because of Homer, the old warriors could never be forgotten, nor could their gods. Another poet, Hesiod, had followed Homer's example and had written down more of the tales of Zeus and the adventures on Mount Olympus. He called his book *Theogony,* "The Doings of the Gods." But Hesiod was a farmer in the back country. "A poor place," he called it, "bad in winter, hard in summer, never good." Planting and the harvest were battles he fought every year. So he wrote about them, too, in *Works and Days,* a farmers' almanac in poetry. He gave advice on when to plow, how to cultivate, and how to prepare for winter. He had suggestions for relaxing in spite of the heat of summer, and made a few cautious remarks about the dangers of sailing as a landlubber saw it.

That was about 700 B.C. A hundred years later, all of Greece had developed an ear for poetry, and it seemed that nearly everyone was writing it. Any intelligent man, in fact, was expected to be able to do it, just as he could play the harp or flute. Politics and laws, love, and history were all set out in verses. Of course, few men were up to writing epic poetry, the long story-poems like those of Homer and Hesiod. And odes, like Pindar's, were for grand occasions and meant to be sung by a chorus. Other people, especially those who wanted to tell of their love or sadness or both, wrote *lyrics.* There were songs sung to the accompaniment of the *lyre,* the little Greek harp.

The most famous of lyric poets was a woman, Sappho, who lived on the island of Lesbos about 590 B.C. It was said that she kept a school for girls, but the Greeks remembered her for her love songs. Years later, historians and other sober-

THIS STATUE OF THE 3RD CENTURY B.C. IS THOUGHT TO BE A PORTRAIT OF SOCRATES.

minded men wrote their thoughts in prose; fewer people wrote poetry. Then, men and girls in love found in Sappho's lyrics the words which expressed their feelings. More than any other poet, she seemed to know what they longed to say themselves. And only she could teach them how to beg Aphrodite not to break their hearts.

GREEK TRAGEDY

In Athens, where poetry turned into plays, poets could be heroes, as honored as the Olympic athletes. In Pericles' time, the contest for playwrights, begun by Pisistratus, became the most exciting event of the year. Even the wars were not allowed to interfere. At the base of the Acropolis, a great new theater was built, big enough for ten or twelve thousand people. On contest days, some spectators arrived before dawn to make certain that they would have seats. By an hour after sunrise, the crowd was pouring into the rows of stone benches, carrying cushions and sandwiches. From their seats, they looked down into the clearing where the old satyr-dances had once been performed. Now it was brushed clean and circled by a ring of white stone. Behind it was the building where the actors changed into their costumes, and beyond, the hills and fields stretched away to the sea.

When the theater was filled, the priests and city officials took their places in the marble seats in the front row. A hush fell over the great crowd and the signal was given for the play to begin. The chorus came on the stage, and then the first of the actors. A large wig and boots with soles several inches thick made him tall. He wore a huge mask, painted to represent his character, so that even the people in the topmost rows could see who he was. When he spoke, a device like a megaphone, built into the mask, let everyone hear.

The play was very different from the acted-out songs which Thespis wrote. There were four actors now, as well as the chorus. Changes of costume and masks allowed them to play many parts. Painted scenery was hung on the actors' dressing house, and from its roof was suspended a "god-machine," the mechanism which "flew" the gods and their messengers above the heads of the other actors.

Such things helped to bring to life the old stories which the plays told. On the clearing below the grandstand, Agamemnon, Hector, Achilles, and Helen of Troy lived once more. Agamemnon came home to his castle at Mycenae, and at the end of his play, he was killed by his treacherous wife. The great doors of the dressing house were flung open to show him lying dead. The chorus, always on stage, watching and commenting, mourned the death of the king and told what it meant to those who still lived in the world of men.

Each morning of the contest, one playwright presented a trilogy—three plays which told three parts of one long story. Since the stories were old, the audience always knew what was going to happen—Agamemnon would die, Troy would fall, or the Trojan women would weep for the loss of their city. The crowd came to see how a new playwright would use the old plot and what new meaning he would find in it.

In the death of kings, there were lessons which touched everyone, but three playwrights could find three different lessons in the same story. Aeschylus, an early playwright, always looked for justice. Some years later, however, Sophocles set out to show his audiences that they must accept life as it was, just or not. Then the wars brought misery to Athens, and another playwright, Euripides, could only write of suffering that seemed cruelly unjust. Each of the three writers won prizes at Athens in his time. Each of them added something of his own to the tragedies, the majestic plays of Greece. And together they won for tragedy a place in the world for all time.

But there was laughter in the theater, too. The contest of plays was still held to honor Dionysus, and no one forgot that he was a god who enjoyed laughing. Tragedy was the morning's business. In the afternoon, the comic playwrights took over. The actors who bounced onto the stage after lunch were much more likely to pretend to be Athenians than heroes. No one was safe from their jokes. They called Pericles "Onion Head" and boastful Cleon "the son of thunder, a robber with the voice of a waterfall." Aristophanes, the greatest of the comic writers, made fun of politicians, sculptors, poets, professors, and ordinary

Athenians sitting in the audience. No over-eager speaker at the Assembly or pompous merchant in the market place escaped his sharp eye. Sooner or later, they turned up in a play. Only in Athens, where men were free to speak their minds, could such a thing have happened. Aristophanes used this right to point out the foolishness and pride which threatened the good of the city.

MOCKING THE GODS

The gods, too, were victims of Aristophanes' humor. In one of his plays, he made the god of war a cook, stirring up a salad—Corinth was the grated cheese and Athens the honey for the dressing. Once he sent an Athenian character up in the "god-machine" to ask the gods for peace. When the man knocked on the door of Zeus' palace, no one was home but Hermes, the messenger. His message was that the gods, tired of humans and their wars, had gone on vacation.

Some people did not laugh at this comedy, because they wondered seriously if the gods were

TRAGEDY AND COMEDY WERE PLAYED AT THE THEATER OF DIONYSOS.

still on Olympus. It had become hard to believe in myths which told of gods who fought each other and perched in clouds. Many Greeks began to doubt that the gods the old poets talked about really existed at all. They still respected the things that the gods stood for—Apollo's discipline and Athena's wisdom. They were sure, too, that some power, strong and good, ruled the world, but it did not matter whether they called it Zeus or Fate or simply God. As for the old myths, they were good stories that helped to explain important ideas. A good example was the tale of the battle of the Lapiths, whose wives were stolen by centaurs, creatures who were half men and half horses. The storytellers said that Apollo helped the Lapiths win the battle and get their wives back. Whether the story was true or not, it taught that the lawlessness of beasts had given way to the order established by men. People were free to believe the myths or not, just as they pleased. If a man said that Apollo had nothing to do with the eclipse of the sun and tried to find out what caused it, no one stopped him.

In Athens in the time of Pericles, men strolled along the paths in the groves beside the playing field and talked. Some of them discussed business, some argued politics—and some had minds that were filled with questions. They had been to school, and they had traveled to other lands. But when they tried to learn the truth about the world around them, there were many facts and few explanations. In the groups that gathered around the benches, they found other men who were troubled by the same difficult questions. "What is the universe?" they asked. "Why does man exist?" Day after day, they argued about the possible answers. If a stranger stopped to listen and asked one of them what they were talking about, he was told: "Philosophy." In Greek, the word meant "the love of wisdom."

Philosophy did not begin in Athens, however,

THE TWO STATUES ARE OF A COMIC ACTOR (LEFT) AND A TRAGIC ACTOR (RIGHT).

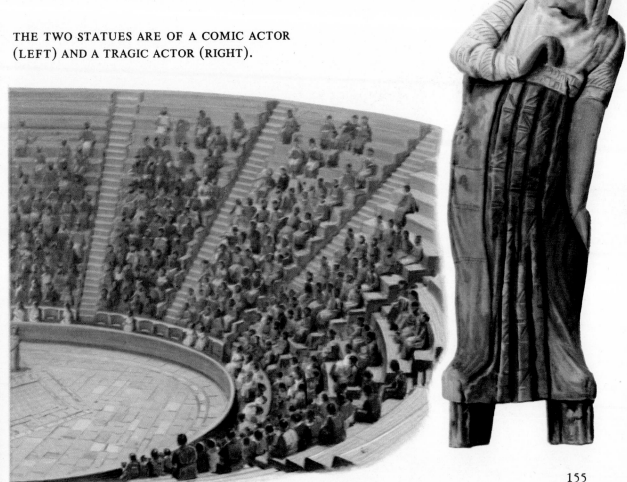

THE GREEK PHILOSOPHERS DISCUSSED THE LAWS
OF NATURE AND THE BEST WAY FOR MEN TO LIVE.

but in Miletus in Asia Minor. There, in the sixth century B.C., a group of men became fascinated with the question: "What is the universe made of?" One philosopher, Thales, suggested that everything was made of water. Another, Anaximenes, noticed that clouds were made of air and eventually became water, so he said that everything was made of air. A third man, Anaximander, disagreed with them both. He said that whatever it was that came first was something invisible, called the "Unlimited," and everything visible came from it.

None of the answers seemed altogether right, perhaps because the men were assuming that the universe was made of just one thing. Nevertheless, they had the courage to ask the question, and they had discovered the way to find the answer— by looking at the world and thinking logically about what was there.

In 585 B.C., Thales believed he knew what caused an eclipse of the sun. He predicted when the next eclipse would happen, and he was right. Then Anaximander built a model of the heavens in order to study the way the planets moved. For the first time, the storytellers, with their tales of the gods, had to face up to scientists.

Meanwhile, a group of men in the Greek cities in Italy had come up with a different kind of

answer to the old riddle of the universe. Mathematics, they said, would explain the world. Their leader, Pythagoras, discovered a basic law of geometry, the Pythagorean Theorem: In any right triangle, the square of the hypotenuse is equal to the sum of the squares of the other two sides. He also noticed that the notes of a musical scale had a mathematical order. When he saw that such different things as music and geometry could be explained by mathematics, he decided that "things are really numbers." Other philosophers answered that mathematics might show how things went together in order, but it did not explain what things really were. And the debate went on.

THE PROBLEM OF CHANGE

In the early fifth century, people began to argue about the problem of change. They wanted to know how something that looked permanent could turn into something else. What really happened, for instance, when a log turned into ashes? Heraclitus, a philosopher from Ephesus, argued firmly that everything was always changing. The nature of the universe was change. "You cannot step into the same river twice," he said, "for new waters are always flowing on." Parmenides, a philosopher from Elea, said just as firmly that Heraclitus was insane; there was no such thing as change. Everything was always the same, but some things merely looked as if they were changing.

To many of the Greeks it seemed that Heraclitus and Parmenides were both wrong. It was common sense that some things change and some do not. Anyone who said it was all one way or the other was simply unreasonable. On the other hand, they had to admit that the arguments which the two men used to back up their ideas seemed reasonable. It was a puzzle, and people began to get discouraged about philosophy. As they wandered from one group of talkers to the next, they heard no reasonable answers. The philosophers could not even agree with each other.

In Pericles' Athens, where a boy learned to argue when he learned to talk, a new group of scholars turned up. They called themselves Sophists, which meant "wise men," and they proclaimed that philosophy was a foolish waste of time. One of them said: "There is no answer to our questions about the world; if there were such an answer, no one would be able to find it; and if someone did find it, he wouldn't be able to explain it to anyone else."

The Sophists set themselves up to teach anything and everything that could be explained. Being practical men, they did it for pay. A few old-fashioned philosophers labeled them "wisdom-peddlers." However, in democratic Athens, where any man could get ahead if he was clever, the Sophists did very well indeed. One of them promised that for a small fee he would teach anyone "the whole duties of man." Another said that he was an expert on arithmetic, geometry, mathematics, grammar, and literature, and was ready to answer any question.

The most important thing the Sophists taught was rhetoric, the art of speaking in a way that persuades people. That was the key to success in the Assembly and the law courts, the places where a young politician could make a name for himself. The Sophists' pupils learned to speak elegant phrases, to argue a point cleverly, and to move the sympathies of a jury. One of the teachers promised that a man who paid his fee and took his course would be able to win any lawsuit. But he changed his guarantee after one of his students refused to pay and suggested that the teacher sue him for the money in the law courts. The young

men who learned from the Sophists embarrassed their elders with clever arguments. So, of course, the elder citizens said that the Sophists were leading the youths astray and ruining Athens.

SOCRATES

About this time, a stone carver named Socrates began to spend his time talking in the market place. He said that his purpose in life was to seek the truth. Soon he had quite a circle of followers, and some of them were young men from the best families in the city. Socrates was bald and had a potbelly, but when he spoke, people forgot what he looked like. His words and his ideas seemed to make everything else unimportant. Athens had never before known such a teacher, and many people wanted the honor of studying with him. But Socrates chose his students carefully. He quickly sent away anyone who was seeking honor rather than learning.

Socrates was a poor man, and his wife was forever nagging him for spending his days talking instead of earning money. Even so, he charged his students no fees. He disliked the Sophists, who taught for pay, and felt that they were giving philosophy a bad reputation. He also thought that the first philosophers had asked the wrong questions, because they began with the universe instead of themselves. "What is man?" asked Socrates. "How can a man lead a good life?"

The good life did not mean riches or fame, but wisdom. A man had to begin by knowing himself. The first step, Socrates said, was admitting that he really knew nothing. He was greatly puzzled when he heard that the Oracle at Delphi had named him as the wisest man in the world, and he set out to find someone wiser in order to prove that the Oracle had made a mistake. In the end, he decided that perhaps she was correct, if she meant that the wisest man in the world was the one who knew just how ignorant he really was.

Socrates became a familiar figure in the market place. Year in, year out, he was there, and always with a cluster of eager students. Even the proud Alcibiades was humble before him. His fame grew, but not his riches. Somehow he managed to scrape together the money for his household bills, and his students saw to it that he was at least well fed. The discussions that started in the market place continued through the evening, at dinner parties where Socrates and his friends talked far into the night. They spoke of the meaning of justice, of friendship, of love, and of courage. There was also much joking, often at Socrates' expense. The tales about his sharp-tongued wife were told time and again, for she had never changed her mind about the time he "wasted" talking.

When Athens went to war, Socrates went, too, and proved to be as good a soldier as he was a philosopher. But the troops remembered him for the time he stood all night in one spot, thinking through an idea.

DEATH OF SOCRATES

After the war, Athens was nervous and afraid. The citizens were suspicious of anything out of the ordinary which might upset things and make them worse than they already were. Socrates was the most extraordinary man in the city; he had earned the hatred of a number of noisy, important men by showing up their ignorance. They began to say that his free way of talking was dangerous, that he had an evil influence on his students. They reminded people that he had taught Alcibiades, who had led Athens to ruin, and Xenophon, who was fighting for the Persians. Eventually Socrates was put on trial before a jury of 501 Athenians. The charge was "failing to believe in the gods of the city, and corrupting the youth of Athens." He was convicted by sixty votes, and the sentence was death. According to custom, he was given a month longer to live. Then he was to kill himself by drinking a poisonous tea brewed from a little plant called the hemlock.

Socrates went on chatting with his friends as eagerly as before. He held firmly to his belief that man had the power to discover the truth. When the time came for him to drink the poison, he still looked for the good. "I am persuaded that it was better for me to die now, and to be released from trouble," he said.

For Athens, the death of Socrates in 399 B.C. was the last and greatest defeat of the war. The people had voted against freedom itself, and condemned wisdom in the name of the goddess who was supposed to guard it.

Socrates had never written down any of his philosophy. But one of his young students, Plato, was determined that his words would not be forgotten. He began to write a series of dialogues, like the conversations which Socrates had had with his friends. First he set down a record of the trial and of his teacher's final days. Then he wrote about Socrates' early life and made certain that no one could mistake him for a Sophist or an enemy of Athens. In the dialogues he described the dinner parties and the walks through the city; the friends who were always there; and the talk that changed the Greeks' way of thinking.

As Plato wrote more dialogues, however, the philosophy gradually became his own and not Socrates'. For men who looked for truth, he had a story. It began with prisoners chained in a cave. Behind them, a bright fire flickered. Between the prisoners and the light of the fire, figures came and went, carrying odd cut-outs of trees and animals and hills. The prisoners, bound so that they faced the wall of their prison, could only see the moving shadows. For them, the shadows were truth. If one of the prisoners was set free, he could turn and see the fire. At first it would be too bright for him to look at it. But when his eyes grew used to the glow, he would walk beyond it to the mouth of his cave. There he would find the sunlight, and again the brightness would blind him. But eventually he would see the real trees and animals and hills—the truth. When he returned to the cave and tried to tell the others what he had seen, they would not believe him. They would laugh or grow angry, as some Athenians did with Socrates. Even so, Plato said, he had to try to explain it to them, to try to set them free.

Plato told the story in the *Republic,* the most famous of his dialogues. There, too, he wrote about his plan for an ideal state. It would be ruled by philosophers, he said, men who were free from the old temptations of power and greed. Its foundations would be the four Greek virtues: courage, temperance, wisdom, and justice.

PLATO'S ACADEMY

In the grove where he and Socrates had walked together, Plato started the Academy, the first university in the western world. His students came from every part of Greece. One of them was Aristotle, a bright seventeen-year-old who turned up in 367 B.C. Plato was sixty then. He and his young pupil made an odd pair when they strolled chatting along the paths. Often they seemed to think as differently as they looked. Plato wanted

CONDEMNED TO DIE FOR HIS BELIEFS, SOCRATES
CARRIED OUT HIS SENTENCE BY DRINKING POISON.

to see the universe all at once. Aristotle wanted to know the secrets of each of its parts. But they shared a love of truth, though they looked for it in different ways. Later they shared a place in the memory of the world as two of the greatest Greek philosophers.

When Plato died in 347 B.C., Aristotle left Athens. But some years later, in 335, he came back to found his own school, the Lyceum. His students soon decided that he lived up to the claims of the Sophist who had boasted that he knew everything. They heard him lecture on one subject after another, and in each he was a master. He gave them their first ideas about biology. He gave them rules for logic, laws for poetry, and others for rhetoric. His first lesson in every subject could be written in one word: "Look." He sent his pupils peering and poking at plants and spiders, at the stars, the sea, and everything around them.

Many of the young philosophers at the Lyceum acted more and more like scientists. In Plato's time, science had been pushed aside. Studying the world of shadows, which was all a scientist could look at, did not seem important. A few scientists had kept at it, of course. Hippocrates had changed the whole idea of medicine by studying symptoms instead of magic. But now Aristotle spoke in favor of science. His lecture notes for astronomy, physics, and biology had enough in them to keep the scientists busy for 1,600 years. They brought him such fame that he was simply called "The Philosopher."

In every subject, the Greeks seemed to lead the world. Never before had people been so certain that they could find what they looked for—the perfect shape for a temple, a first prize at the Olympics, a good life, or the truth about the universe. Like the little city-states, each man went his own way. For the cities, that brought squabbles, wars, and disaster. But for men, it meant freedom and the courage to try out their new ideas. "We must follow where the arguments lead us," Socrates had said, and in two thousand years the world was still following the paths which the Greeks had discovered.

The Conquerors

343 B.C.-323 B.C.

IN 343 B.C., the philosopher Aristotle left the quiet of his study and journeyed to Macedonia, a country in the mountain wilderness north of Greece. He had been hired to tutor the rowdy young son of the king. The boy, Alexander, was a yellow-haired thirteen-year-old. His manners were polite and he seemed to be clever enough, but he was wild. It was hard for him to pay attention to his studies. He much preferred galloping across the fields on his huge war horse. He proudly told his new tutor that he had tamed the horse himself. When he did come to his lessons, instead of discussing arithmetic and Greek grammar, he chatted on about armies and his father's campaigns and his own great plans to conquer the world.

Alexander said that he was a descendant of the family of Achilles—his mother had told him so. The *Iliad,* Achilles' story, was the one book he loved. He carried it with him wherever he went, and read it over and over until he knew it by heart. He dreamed of growing up to be a hero like the ones in Homer's poem. He pestered Aristotle with questions about Greece and Athens, which he longed to visit. Aristotle said that it was very different from Macedonia.

PHILIP OF MACEDON

In those days Macedonia was just beginning to be a kingdom that civilized people talked about seriously. The Greeks still said it was a country of barbarians, but the Greeks called everyone who

wasn't Greek a barbarian. Macedonia was changing. Alexander's father, King Philip, had spent his youth as a hostage in Greece, and he had learned to love almost everything Greek. He had studied the language and tried to learn the ways of the people. But he had also heard the Greeks laugh at the rough peasants of his homeland. When he was set free and went home to become a king, he determined to make Macedonia a country that no one could laugh at again. He turned his peasants into well-trained soldiers, and conquered the lands east and west of his kingdom, as far as the Danube and the Hellespont. Then he went back to Greece.

Greece, too, had changed. It was more than fifty years since Sparta had defeated Athens and set itself up as the new "protector" of all Greece. There had been more wars, for Sparta could only do things in its own way, and the other cities preferred any way but that one. The council which the Spartans appointed to govern Athens ruled by murder and taxed by robbery. In other places, it was worse. Then the king of Persia picked a quarrel with the Spartans. They fought, and the Persians won all the Greek cities in Asia Minor.

That was the signal for the mainland Greeks to try to revolt against Sparta. Thebes, a big city

ALEXANDER THE GREAT, DEPICTED IN A ROMAN MOSAIC COPIED FROM A GREEK PAINTING, BUILT A VAST EMPIRE BY CONQUEST.

in the north, declared war. Then the Thebans defeated a strong force of the best Spartans, but the sides were so evenly matched that neither could force the other to surrender. Darkness, not victory, ended the fighting. The leaders counted their losses and had no heart to attack again in the morning. They knew that the wars could go on forever. The Greeks would be divided and open to attack from Persia, because no one city was strong enough to hold the others together.

That was the way things were when Philip of Macedonia returned to Greece. He came, he said, as a friend, but his troops were right behind him. He took some land and cities by force, but he also helped the Thebans rescue Delphi and its sacred temples from a band of invaders. For that he won the friendship of the priests and the right to call himself a Greek. Now, wherever Philip went, he spoke of his love for Greece and his fellow Greeks. He said that it was his dream to lead them against the Persians in Asia Minor, and he suggested that they might like to join him in a new, strong Greek league.

DEMOSTHENES

To many Greeks, Philip looked like the man who might save them. Others said so because he had paid them to. One of these hired men got up to speak before the Assembly at Athens, hoping to convince the citizens that the king of Macedonia was really a Greek at heart. He told them that Philip was a fine speaker, beautiful to look at, and a good companion over a cup of wine. Another speaker, a man named Demosthenes, interrupted him and climbed onto the platform.

"As to these becoming qualities," Demosthenes began, "I do not see that they add up to a Greek or to a worthy commander. The first, fine speech, becomes any speaker; the second, good looks, becomes a woman; and the third, that King Philip soaks up wine, can be matched by any sponge."

Nowhere in Greece did Philip have a more determined enemy than this Demosthenes. He was the finest orator in Athens, a city where men spent their lives learning to speak well. In his youth, Demosthenes was not a good speaker. It was said that he trained himself to form words clearly by practicing speaking with pebbles in his mouth. He had made his voice strong by reciting verses above the sound of ocean waves. He never ran short of breath, for he had taught himself to speak while he was running or climbing a steep hill. And he still practiced in front of a mirror the gestures and movements that held everyone's attention when he mounted the platform at the Pnyx.

Week after week, Demosthenes used all his talents in a campaign of words against King Philip. He reminded the Athenians about the ancient heroes who had fought for Greece. He asked them how they, descendants of such noble men, could welcome this new invader instead of fighting him. But it was as difficult for Demosthenes to persuade the citizens of Athens to go to war as it had once been for Nicias to talk them out of it. They listened and cheered—they were very fond of good speeches—but they delayed. They would not vote against Philip, nor would they vote for him.

In 338 B.C., Philip grew tired of waiting and led his soldiers into central Greece. At last the Athenians took Demosthenes' advice. They joined Thebes in raising an army to stop the invaders. It was a brave defense, but hopeless. Philip's well-drilled troops were fresh and strong, while the Greeks were worn out from many years of war. The Thebans and Athenians were badly defeated. Demosthenes could ask no more of them. He kept silent while the Greeks, for the first time, swore their obedience to a foreign king.

Philip was full of plans for the great invasion of Persia, but the campaign was never begun. A jealous member of his Macedonian court stabbed him while he was marching, unarmed, in a procession. A day later, he was dead. In Athens the citizens hung themselves with garlands and paraded through the streets chanting hymns of joy. Philip was gone, his son was barely twenty years old, and the oaths to obey the king of Macedonia could be forgotten.

ALEXANDER THE GREAT

For two years the Greeks heard little of Alexander. They ignored his laws and made jokes about the little groups of Macedonian soldiers which were still scattered about Greece. But when the Thebans attacked the Macedonians in their city, the young king swooped down on Thebes like the god of thunder. He destroyed the city, killed 6,000 of its people, and sold the rest into slavery. He left nothing to mark the spot where

THE GREAT ORATOR DEMOSTHENES TRIED TO ROUSE THE PEOPLE AGAINST PHILIP OF MACEDONIA.

Thebes had been, except the sacred temples and the house of the poet Pindar. The citizens of the other Greek cities thought again and decided that it was wise not to question Alexander's youth or his authority.

ALEXANDER'S CAMPAIGNS

Aristotle's pupil had become a handsome and rugged soldier, who looked like the Achilles he longed to be. At twenty, he was already a more skillful general than his father had been, and his mind was full of campaign plans. Philip had loved Greece, so much that he wanted all of it. But Aristotle had taught Alexander to love the world. For him, Greece was only a beginning.

In the spring of 334 B.C., Alexander led a force of 30,000 Macedonian and Greek soldiers and 5,000 cavalrymen across the Hellespont, the channel which divided the western world from the East. Once Xerxes and his Persians had crossed this boundary on the way to invade Greece. Now it was the Greeks' turn, and Persia was their goal. On a hill above the Hellespont, at the spot where Troy had stood, Alexander halted his troops. He visited an ancient Greek temple and prayed to Athena to guard his soldiers. He

163

set a crown on the grave of his hero, Achilles. Then he gave the order to march on.

Meanwhile, Darius III, King of Persia, had been warned about the invasion. The number of enemy troops seemed small to him. He laughingly told his advisers that the young Macedonian sounded more impertinent than dangerous. He sent a reliable unit of Persians to stop the invaders at the river Granichus, not far from Troy. He saw no reason to go himself. These little wars were not unusual in his huge empire, and he always won them.

Darius' soldiers were waiting when Alexander reached the river. They had a strong position and knew that he, like any other commander, would take a day or two to plan his attack. But

Alexander was not like any other commander. When he saw the enemy line, he gave a shout and led his cavalry across the water in a wild charge that scattered the startled Persians and sent them flying for safety. His foot soldiers waded across to mop up the stragglers, and that was the end of the battle.

THE MACEDONIAN PHALANX

After that, speed was a weapon Alexander used often. He fired his huge troop of cavalry into the center of enemy lines like a spear, and always the enemy soldiers broke in confusion. But he was also ready for the tough, close-in

ALEXANDER'S ROUTE FROM MACEDONIA TO THE INDUS
AND HIS MARCH BACK ACROSS THE DESERT

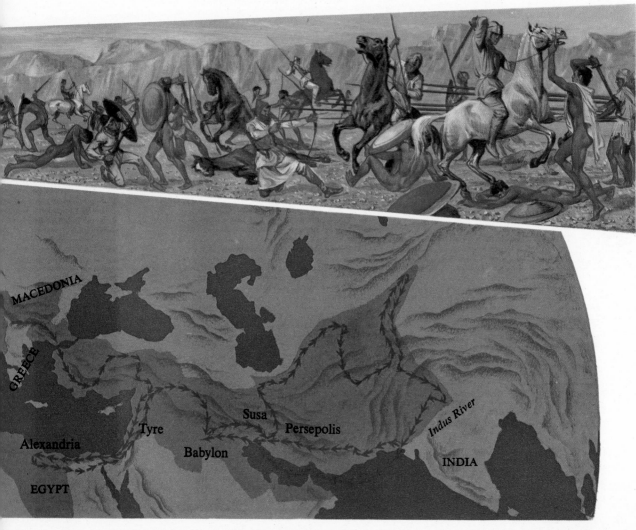

fighting, when it was soldier against soldier and the lines of infantry hacked across the field by inches. For that part of the battle Alexander had the famous Macedonian Phalanx. This was a mass of infantry so many lines deep that no enemy charge could break through it. The well-drilled soldiers fought together like a machine. In defense, they made the phalanx a wall without a single gap. In attack, they were a battering ram of men. And Alexander had another weapon, one which his enemies could not match—the love and loyalty of his soldiers. He did not send them into battle; he led them, and they never failed him.

DARIUS FLEES

City after city surrendered to Alexander's soldiers as he took them south through Asia Minor. In less than a year, he had reached Syria. There, at Issus, a narrow plain bounded by mountains and ocean, he came upon the main Persian army. King Darius had come himself, this time, for he intended to smash the invaders once and for all. He stood proudly in his chariot at the center of the line, surrounded by his hand-picked bodyguard, the finest soldiers in Persia. Alexander aimed his cavalry at that spot. The horsemen thundered across the field and the line splintered. Darius leaped from his chariot, grabbed a horse, and rode furiously for safety. His startled soldiers ran in every direction, and Alexander's men were still chasing them at sunset.

That night, the tired visitors made themselves comfortable in the splendid tents and pavilions of Darius' camp. Alexander moved into the king's own tent. He bathed himself in the royal bath, with its water pots and ointment boxes all of heavy gold. Then, scented with Persian bath oil, he wandered into the great pavilion and found the elegant couches and silver-inlaid tables arranged for a banquet. He sprawled across a cushiony couch, reached for a pear and a cup of wine, and sighed: "This, it seems, is royalty."

Alexander enjoyed being royalty. When he had pushed his way into Egypt, he sailed up the Nile in a gilded barge, nodding to the people who lined the shore and called him "liberator." At the place where the river meets the Mediterranean, he founded a city and named it for himself, Alexandria. Then he made the long journey across the desert to the temple of Amon, the Egyptian Zeus. There the priests met him, crying, "Welcome, son of Zeus, thy godly father greets thee!"

That made Alexander a god on earth, at least in Egypt. He enjoyed that, too. He began to dress and act more like the Oriental kings, whose subjects knelt to them and called them lord. Some of his old friends were angered to discover that he expected the men who fought by his side in battle to treat him reverently when he sat on his throne. On the field, however, he was the same Alexander who had galloped across the hills of Macedonia. When King Darius made an offer of peace if Alexander would agree to divide the Eastern world with him, he refused. He left the pleasures of Egypt behind and marched his men back to Syria, determined to take Babylon.

THE BATTLE OF GAUGEMELA

Not long after he had crossed the Euphrates River, his scouts rode in to report a gigantic collection of armies camped on the plain at Gaugamela. Alexander waved his troops to a halt, while he and his generals rode to a hill to survey the enemy camp. Soldiers and equipment covered the plain and the low-lying hills. There were Persian foot soldiers by the thousands, the royal bodyguard, troops from central Asia, and the cavalry of a dozen nations. There was also a long line of Persian chariots with sharp blades, like scythes, fastened to their sides. When they charged, the blades would slice through entire files of soldiers.

Alexander returned to his troops. He ordered them to make camp, and gave them a day to rest and prepare for the battle. The next night he rode to the hill again. In the flickering light of thousands of campfires he saw the Persians, already arming. One of his generals suggested he attack while it was still dark, to surprise and confuse the enemy. Alexander glared angrily at the man. "I steal no victories," he said, and went back to his camp to wait for the dawn.

In the morning, he led his men onto the field at Gaugamela. The wings of the enemy lines were spread so wide that it seemed they could defeat him just by folding in and trapping his army. But Alexander had put extra guards on the flanks, and he hoped that once the fight had begun, some of those far-spread Persian units would have to run to defend the center. For once, he did not charge; he waited for the enemy to come at him. The first to move were the scythe-chariots, wheeling in from the side, aiming to slice through the ranks. But the Macedonian archers peppered them with arrows, and grabbed for the horses' reins as the chariots came nearer. The men in the phalanxes simply stepped aside, on command, and let the chariots rattle past.

DEATH OF DARIUS

The Persian center charged, with Darius in the lead. Alexander spotted a gap in the line and rushed his horsemen into it. He turned and beat his way along the line. Now the troops on the Persian wing dashed in to protect the center. The flying white plumes on Alexander's helmet disappeared in the crush of soldiers, shields, and banners. Suddenly, Darius' chariot shot out of the tumult. His soldiers gasped when they saw him race from the field and away. The Persian line crumpled, then burst, as the men tried to flee the Macedonian cavalry. Though many of the Asians fought on until dark, the outcome of the battle had been decided when Darius ran. The field at Gaugamela and all of Persia belonged to Alexander.

The gates of Babylon were thrown open for him without a fight. For a time, he made the city his home, living in the royal splendor of the Persian king's winter palace. Darius himself had disappeared. Alexander tracked him down, only to find that he had been killed by some of his own officers.

The next year, 330 B.C., Alexander set out to conquer and explore the enormous eastern empire which he had won. He roamed across Iran and south through the Indus, followed by a city of tents. His camp was his court and the capital of Persia. Behind the soldiers came officials and clerks, engineers and doctors, money-changers, poets, athletes, and jesters. In the evenings, when the camp had been set up, there were races and wrestling, or contests for the musicians. The men chatted over bowls of wine, as though they were still in Greece or Babylon. But in the morning, they folded up their city and moved on. For five years, Alexander wandered through the strange, half-known countries of his empire. Then his men would go no

WHEN DARIUS FLED IN HIS CHARIOT FROM THE BATTLE AT GAUGAMELA, ALL PERSIA FELL TO ALEXANDER.

farther. They had roamed enough and begged him to take them back to Babylon.

The march home took two years more. The caravan made its way along the shore of the Indian Ocean, followed by the fleet which Alexander had built in the Indus. The last stretch of the journey was across a desert wasteland. The water ran out, food was scarce, and there were many deaths. But, at last, the great caravan reached Babylon.

Alexander had learned to love the eastern world, which called him a god. Now, as he began to set his empire in order, he said that it must be both Asian and Greek, an empire in which the nations of East and West shared their best with each other. In his travels he had founded many cities, Greek cities. He had provided the gold for 30,000 Persian youths to be educated in the Greek way and taught the things which he had learned from Aristotle. But in his court, he had Persian officials as well as Greeks and Macedonians. He married a Persian princess and insisted that his officers also take oriental wives. A great festival was proclaimed to celebrate the wedding of East and West.

ALEXANDER DIES

Alexander talked about adding Africa and the western Mediterranean to his world. It would take no fewer than a thousand ships of war, he said, and he would build a highway to carry his troops across the top of Africa. Then, in the spring of 323 B.C., he fell sick with a fever. He knew that there would be no more campaigns. He had never spared himself in battle, and now the old wounds added to his weakness. He asked that his soldiers be allowed to visit him. As he lay propped up on his couch, the men who had come with him from Greece and Macedonia filed through his chamber. They mumbled their farewells and marched on.

A few days later Alexander died. He was not yet thirty-three and his hair was still yellow, but he would go down in history as Alexander the Great.

Greece and the World

323 B.C.- 250 B.C.

IN THE last years of the fourth century B.C., Greek citizens going about their business in the *stoas* or the shops sometimes stopped and wondered what was wrong. Everything seemed strange. They themselves had not changed, and their cities looked the same as before, but the world around them was so different that they could hardly recognize themselves.

The little *poleis* on the mainland looked out at an enormous empire, which stretched across Asia and Egypt. They shipped their olive oil and pottery across the Mediterranean. Their corn came from fields beside the Black Sea and the Nile. Merchants who crowded their market places now did business in Antioch, and their sculptors had gone to Alexandria. There were new Greek cities, thousands of miles from Greece, where Asians spoke Greek and Greeks began to dress like the barbarians. But there were no barbarians now, only the many sorts of people who shared

THE AGORA, OR MARKETPLACE, OF ATHENS WITH A STOA, OR COVERED WALK. AT LEFT, A BRONZE HEAD OF APHRODITE FROM THE 2ND CENTURY B.C.

a world which Alexander had conquered for the Greeks. As the world the Greeks knew became larger, a man and his city seemed to become smaller. And the Greeks began to wonder if there was a Greece at all any more.

Athenians who traveled on business saw Athens in a new way when they came home. It was not very big and not very busy. When they went to the Assembly, the fine speeches had a hollow ring. In the old days, when Pericles or Themistocles spoke to the Assembly, things happened and the world felt the difference. But now, a man who spoke out in Athens might as well have dropped a pebble in an ocean.

Alexander's empire was much too big to be run by a group of citizens who talked over their problems in an Assembly. But one man could rule it, if he was a king like Alexander and had a strong army. When Alexander died, the strongest of his generals split the empire into three pieces, each bigger by far than Greece. Each was ruled by a despot, an all-powerful king whose word was law to millions of people who would never see him.

In Egypt, the sons of the general Ptolemy began to call themselves Pharaohs and gods. The Seleucids, another military family, took most of the old Persian lands. Macedonia and Greece were claimed by the general Antigonus.

The Athenians were ready to fight for their independence, but they knew that their city was too small, too weak, and too tired to hold off a despot's well-drilled army. Worse than that, they realized that Athens was old-fashioned. In the empire that Alexander had left behind, a city that acted like a country was a joke.

At the barber shop or the Assembly, the talk was always the same. "Fifteen years ago . . ." someone would say, and the others would nod in agreement. "Yes, fifteen years ago, a citizen of Athens knew where he stood."

Fifteen years ago, before Alexander had changed the world, the *polis* had been everything. A citizen was protected by it, and worked for it, taking on jobs in the government. His life was comfortable and he lived with honor. If he wrote a story, composed a song, or carved a statue, he did it for the glory of Athens, and earned a little glory for himself, too. Now Athens did not matter. Nothing was glorious.

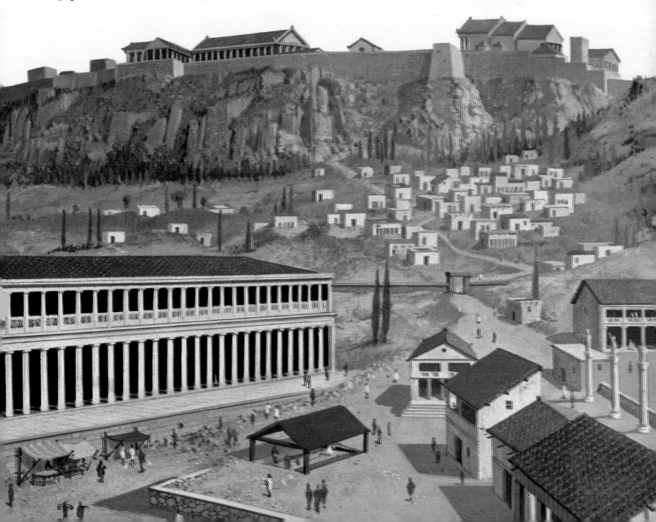

The talkers would shake their heads and wander away to talk to other men, who would say the same things again. Alexander had promised to win a world for them. Instead, he had taken away the one world they knew. The Greek *poleis* were dying, and Demosthenes' strong and independent Greece was already dead.

Many of the Greeks found comfort in thinking of the good old days, when Greece had been the home of heroes. They read Homer again and filled their houses with statues and paintings of his warriors. They learned to sing old folk songs and collected antiques—bits of rusty armor and old pottery. They did not care what it was, so long as it reminded them that once the Greeks had been powerful and life had been good.

Some Greeks looked to the gods for help. Day after day, chanting and the piping of flutes filled the streets, as hundreds of men and women followed the priests to the temples. They made their sacrifices, tried to obey the laws of their religion, and hoped that when they died they would be taken to the "Isles of the Blessed," where heroes lived forever.

THE ASIAN GODS

But it was hard to believe that the old gods on Olympus cared what happened to men. The gods of Asia made better promises, and many Greeks turned to them. Some of the new gods were beautiful, like the Egyptian Isis with her gentle eyes. Some, like the sun god Amon, were frightening. But all of them could foretell the future, and all of them guaranteed their followers a happier life in a paradise that was just the other side of death. That was cheering news to the Greeks who were frightened of the future and dissatisfied with their life on earth. They flocked to the shrines of the new gods, luck charms around their necks, and forgot their cares in dreams of the wonderful life after death.

In the meantime, the once plain-living Greeks were taking an interest in fine clothes, fancy furniture, and banquets. If their cities no longer gave them important things to do or think about, they could at least spend their time enjoying themselves. They began to listen to music and poetry just because it was beautiful, and delighted in stories that made them laugh instead of teaching them a lesson.

A new kind of comedy was playing at the theater. Politics was no longer a laughing matter, but Athenians could laugh at themselves—or, better still, at the fellow next door. Menander, the best of the new playwrights, kept Athens chuckling at the funny things which might have happened in any house in the city. There were pinch-penny fathers with sharp-tongued wives and girl-crazy sons who tried to trick them out of their money. Sly servants got everything into a tangle, then stopped to tell jokes, and the audience howled.

But serious-minded citizens saw little to laugh at anywhere. The people walking in the groves beside the playing fields wore long faces and their talk was gloomy. Once they had listened to men like Plato and Aristotle. They had hoped then to understand everything in the universe. Now they hoped for nothing, and listened only to teachers who told them how to make the best of things.

One group, a circle of men who called themselves the Cynics, said that the only way to get along was to play it safe. Their first teacher, Antisthenes, recalled that Socrates had said: "Nothing which does not make a man worse can hurt him." So Antisthenes and his students set out to avoid anything that might make them worse. Money was the first thing they put on the list, then art, science, poetry, politics, and music. Each time they talked together, the list of things grew longer, but they were proud to say that they were learning to do without them all.

DIOGENES

With their untrimmed beards and ragged clothes, the Cynics were a sour-faced, odd-looking lot. The oddest of them all was Diogenes of Synope, who did without almost everything. It was said that he gave up his house and lived in a clay jar about the size of a bathtub. People told of meeting him roaming the streets in broad daylight with a lighted lamp. Diogenes explained that he was searching for an honest man. When Alexander had once visited Athens, he wanted to see this strange philosopher who said that the world's riches were hateful. He found Diogenes sunning himself in the market place and offered to do him a favor, anything he asked for. Diogenes looked up at the great conqueror. "A favor?" he said. "Yes. Move over—you're cutting off my sunlight."

EPICURUS AND HIS STUDENTS IN HIS GARDEN OUTSIDE ATHENS

A very different kind of man was Epicurus, a teacher who chatted with his students every afternoon in a quiet garden outside the city. Epicurus said that Diogenes and the Cynics had the wrong idea altogether. "What is the use of trying to make life safe by running away from everything that makes life good?" he asked.

There were no sour faces in Epicurus' garden, for he told his students that the secret of a good life was learning to enjoy life's pleasures. While the men sprawled on the grass and talked together pleasantly, like old friends, he tried to teach them to avoid the things that could spoil their pleasures. He especially tried to teach them not to be afraid. Most men feared death and what came after, but Epicurus said that they were wrong to be frightened. He told his students that when people died, the atoms of which they were made sprang apart. Then they did not exist, so they could not be hurt, and need not be afraid. But they had every good reason to enjoy things while they were still alive.

"Eat, drink, and be merry, for tomorrow you die!" was the way some people put it, and used this philosophy as an excuse to be greedy. But that was not what Epicurus meant at all. He warned his students that too many pleasures were as bad as none at all. "Pick and choose," he said. "Art, poetry, knowledge, and good friends are pleasures that will not fail. Anger, greed, and fear can be avoided. Wisdom, like our garden wall, will shut them out."

ZENO THE STOIC

But there were some men in Athens who had no wish to hide behind garden walls. They went to listen to Zeno, a young man who had come to the city as a merchant and stayed to be a philosopher. Zeno's friends were statesmen, officers, and men of affairs. Their meeting place was a *stoa* in the busy market, and so they were called the Stoics. Zeno said he was tired of hearing Athenians whine that they had no strength or freedom because their city was weak. He told them they had a strength of their own, in their ability to reason like men. He reminded them that no tyrant could really conquer their wills. When people came to Zeno with fears or sorrows, he told them to forget them, because such things simply did not matter. And he tried to teach them why this was so.

"There is a wise god," Zeno said, "who has the plan of history in his mind. The plan is like an endless story, with a little tale about every nation, man, or insect that will ever exist. We men can never understand the whole story, but we can use our reason to discover our own tales, the tasks which are ours to do. When we find them,

171

it is our duty to do them well, and to meet every hardship with one thought: 'If it is God's will, it is my will, too.' Then pain and grief will not matter. We can ignore them." It was easy to say and hard to do. A man needed a strong will indeed to remind himself that a pain which tortured him did not matter because it was only part of a plan. But Zeno's ideas gave courage to men who had begun to feel small. Many Athenians became Stoics. They squared their shoulders and showed the great new world that there were some Greeks in it who were not afraid.

But those who were ambitious did not stay long in Athens. They followed the crowds to Antioch and Alexandria and the other big cities across the Mediterranean. These cities, built by Alexander, were not like Athens. None of them tried to be a country or called itself a *polis*. The new word was *cosmopolis,* "a city of the world."

Passengers bound for Alexandria could tell, long before their ships reached port, that they were coming to a place like none they had known before. During the night, far out on the sea, they caught sight of the bright beam of light from the beacon in the harbor. When they docked in the morning, they passed the lighthouse itself, looming above them, forty stories high. It was a wonder of design and engineering, but it was only an introduction to Alexander's first and greatest city.

ALEXANDRIA

The streets of Alexandria were straight and long. Two avenues, a hundred feet wide, crossed at the city's center. They were lined with porches, whose roofs were held up by endless rows of columns. Visitors strolling in the cool shade of the porches could see above them the royal palaces and the magnificent Mausoleum, where the body of Alexander lay in an alabaster coffin. If the strangers' business was official, they would enter one of the huge blocks of government offices, just off the avenue. Otherwise, they might refresh themselves after their journey with exercise in a gymnasium or a swim and a snack at the public baths.

A SARCOPHAGUS OF AN EGYPTIAN GREEK

Wherever the visitors went, they heard a babble of languages, for Alexandria was the trading center of the world. The people of Africa, Asia, and Europe mingled in its streets. They traded together in its market place and warehouses, lived side by side, and forgot that their nations had once been separate. That had been Alexander's dream. When he had planned his city, he had set aside space for temples to honor the gods of Greece, but he also made room for shrines to the Egyptian goddess Isis. He started the famous Library, where the books of

173

Greece and Asia were collected, and he built the Museum—a temple of the Muses—that became an international university.

EXPLORING SCIENCE

In Alexandria, people were interested in practical things—weights and numbers, dollars and cents, shapes and sizes. The scholars at the Museum looked at things in the same way. They were scientists, practical men who looked for practical methods of finding answers to the most difficult questions. They asked: How big is the moon? How small is the tiniest living thing? What is the earth made of?

Many of their questions had never been asked before. The scientists were explorers, searching out the mysteries of the world in which man lived. There were no maps to guide them, but Aristotle had left them a kind of rough sketch. He had marked off the territories, the kingdoms of animals, medicine, stars, and the rest. His students had learned to look and measure and count. "First put things in order," he had told them. "See how they fit together."

One of Aristotle's pupils, Theophrastus, was still in Athens, examining the strange Asian leaves and flowers which Alexander had ordered his scientists to collect for his old teacher. Theophrastus set the odd plants side by side, studying their likenesses and differences, and tried to discover how they were related.

The scientists at Alexandria studied other regions of knowledge. There was no Plato to tell them to fit everything into one great picture of the universe. Instead, each man had his field, and the more he studied, the more details he found to interest and excite him. Every science seemed to be as complicated as a universe.

Plato's student Euclid came to the Museum to work out his laws of geometry. Then he put his lessons into a book, the *Elements*, and the job was done for all time. His young pupils always hoped there might be some easier way to learn geometry. But when they complained, Euclid added one more law to the list: "There is no royal road to geometry."

Scientists in other territories had trouble finding their roads at all. Often their greatest discoveries came by accident. Archimedes of Syracuse stepped into his bath one morning and

ERATOSTHENES, AN ALEXANDRIAN ASTRONOMER AND MATHEMATICIAN, DREW A MAP OF THE KNOWN WORLD.

ARCHIMEDES DEMONSTRATING HIS SYSTEM OF PULLEYS AND GEARS

noticed that as he sat down the water rose higher in the tub. He lifted out one foot, and the water went down slightly. He plunged his foot back into the water, and again the water rose. He tried it several times, then suddenly he bellowed, *"Eureka*—I have found it!" His servants, sure that he was drowning, rushed in to save him. But Archimedes smiled at them over the edge of the tub. He had just discovered a way to measure the weight of ships. It could be done by calculating the weight of the water displaced by a floating ship.

A bathtub was as good as most of the makeshift tools which the Museum's scientists had to work with. They had no lenses for microscopes and telescopes, no thermometers, no equipment for measuring things accurately. But they put together gadgets of string, sticks, and bits of bronze, and got on with their investigations. When Archimedes went home to Syracuse, he was able to dumbfound his king with his discoveries. He rigged a series of pulleys which allowed the king to hoist a ship onto a dock simply by turning a crank. Then he showed him how to use a pole as

DETAIL OF ARCHIMEDES' WOODEN GEARS

175

a lever to move a rock which eight men could not lift with their hands.

Another scientist, Erastosthenes, was able to estimate the size of the earth by measuring the shadows made by the sun at two places in Egypt, 700 miles apart. Then Aristarchus of Samos went to work on a method for measuring the sizes and distances of the sun and moon. But none of the other scholars paid much attention to him, because he had the crazy idea that the sun was the center of the universe and the earth revolved. It was nearly 2,000 years before astronomers found out that he was right.

In the meantime, everyone followed the ideas of the greatest of the Museum's stargazers and map makers, a man who was called Ptolemy, though he was not of the Egyptian kings' family. Ptolemy mapped out the universe with the earth

ARCHIMEDES' SCREW, WHEN FITTED INTO A CYLINDER, WAS USED TO RAISE WATER TO A HIGHER LEVEL.

neatly in the center, surrounded by the planets and stars. There were more than a thousand stars on the map, most of them discovered and named —without the help of a telescope—by Hipparchus, an astronomer at Rhodes.

Hipparchus made many discoveries. He was the first man to figure out the exact length of a year by watching the movements of the sun. And he invented the lines of latitude and longitude which the geographers used when they drew maps of the earth. The new maps were big, for explorers were roaming far now. Some of the reports they brought back from their expeditions were not easy to believe. When Ptolemy made a world map to go with his map of the universe, he put in the Atlantic Ocean and the newly discovered islands of Britain. But he refused to include the "Sea of Jelly," the sailors' name for an ocean crusted with ice which they had found far in the north. A man who knew only the warm waters of the Mediterranean could not imagine such a thing.

While the philosophers stayed in Athens and the scientists in Alexandria, the artists of Greece raced from place to place, trying to keep up with their orders. There was little work for them in Athens, but the rich new trading centers across the sea were eager to put up fine buildings and decorate their streets. When the architects and sculptors arrived, the orders were always the same: "It doesn't matter what it costs, but make it better than Athens."

THE COLOSSUS OF RHODES

The merchants of Rhodes, a wealthy island crossroads in the Aegean, spent their gold for great marble buildings and 3,000 statues by the finest sculptors. At the entrance to their harbor, they raised a mammoth bronze figure of the sun god, ten stories high. It was called the Colossus of Rhodes. But Rhodes was outdone by Pergamum, a town in Asia Minor that came to be called the most beautiful city in the world.

From a distance, the Acropolis at Pergamum looked like a city of the gods that might suddenly disappear in a cloud. Closer, it was even more lovely. The Acropolis rose 900 feet in a series of terraces, with buildings of white marble set in gardens. There were statues everywhere. Many of them honored a tribe of barbarians whom the soldiers of Pergamum had defeated in battle.

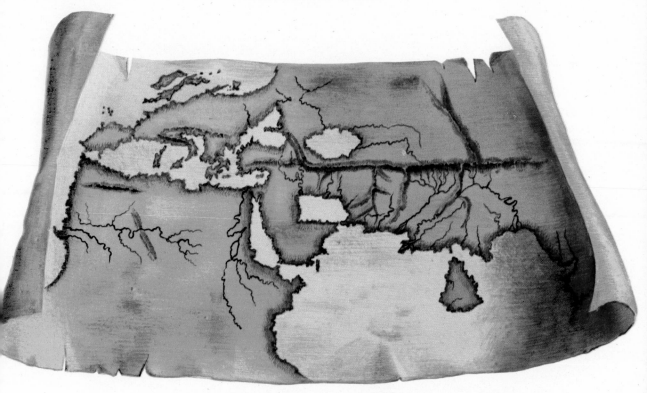

PTOLOMY'S MAP OF THE WORLD

In figures of bronze and marble, the fierce warriors fought again, so real that it was hard to believe that the tensed muscles could not move or that the faces, pulled tight with pain, could never change.

THE ALTAR OF ZEUS

The wonder of Pergamum was the Altar of Zeus. There, the battle of the gods and giants was shown in a great carving, seven feet high and four hundred feet long. Many people said the sculpture was finer than the one at Athens which showed the same battle. There was an important difference, however. The sculpture at Athens was meant to do more than tell a story. It was supposed to remind the citizens of the struggle between human order and the stupidity of beasts. The splendid carvings at Pergamum only told the story.

Most artists only told the story now. That was what people wanted, statues that were beautiful and seemed real. They praised the softness of Athena's mantle when they looked at Phidias' carving in the Parthenon. They were even more impressed with the statue of an athlete carved by another Athenian, Polyclitus. He and his friend Praxiteles became famous for the grace and naturalness of their statues. Then the Greeks discovered Scopas, a sculptor who showed pain and grief so perfectly that people looked for the tears in the eyes of his statues. Love, sorrow, and death became the sculptors' subjects.

Painters, too, tried to copy real things exactly. In Athens, two artists held a contest to see which of them could make the most realistic painting. Zeuxis painted a bunch of grapes which looked so real that birds flew down to peck at them. Parrhasius, his rival, looked at the wonderful painting, went home, and a few days later invited Zeuxis to come and see a picture he had made. When Zeuxis, still proud of his grapes, walked into his friend's studio, Parrhasius pointed to a painting covered by a curtain. Zeuxis walked over, reached up to draw the curtain, then quickly pulled his hand away. He had lost the contest, for the curtain he touched was the painting.

Those who could afford them hurried to buy such marvelously real statues and paintings— portraits of the heroes, of famous men like Alexander, or of the gods in all their beauty. It

THE ALTAR OF ZEUS AT PERGA-
MUM, AND A STATUE OF THE 3RD
CENTURY B.C.

did not occur to the buyers that some of the new
figures had been made to stand oddly, as though
the artists were only trying to show off their
cleverness. They did not notice that sometimes the
statues were too graceful and elegant. Like many
Greeks, the artists were looking backward to the
great old days, when men were almost gods.
But they remembered only what was pretty and
forgot what was strong.

That was happening everywhere in the Greek
world. Poets tried to write like Homer and
Pindar. The stories were the same, but the new
poems were failures. The only fine poet in all of
Alexandria was Theocritus, who had better sense
than to make imitations. He invented his own
kind of poetry, which he called the *pastoral*. In
the rush of the city, he wrote about his homeland,
Sicily; and delighted the worldly-wise Alexandrians with his tales of sunny meadows, cheerful
shepherds, and romantic youths and girls.

Perhaps the Alexandrians were fond of the

stories because they told about a charming world
that was no longer real, like the world of Greece.
That world, once real, was gone. It had disappeared with Pericles, Socrates, and the strength
of the little *poleis* that had worn themselves out.
Now it lived only in statues, plays, and books.
Over 700,000 volumes were jammed into the
great Library at Alexandria. Scholars pored over
them. Scribes copied them so that libraries in all
the new cities could have them. Every educated
person read them, for the new world was learning
Greek.

Centuries later, the people of the other new
worlds would also learn Greek. They would read
Homer and put up theaters for the plays from
Athens. They would build temples which they
hoped were like the ones on the Acropolis. They
would run marathon races at their own Olympic
Games, and study science according to Aristotle's
rules. Sometimes they would think about the puzzle of Greece: a little nation that was never a
nation at all had somehow conquered the minds
of the world for all time. And they would
remember Pericles, who once told his Athenians:
"Future ages will wonder at us, for our adventurous spirit has taken us to every sea and country,
and everywhere we have left behind us ever-
lasting monuments."

GREEK STATUE OF 4TH OR 3RD CENTURY B.C., ONE OF MANY FOUND IN THE TOMBS AT THE TOWN OF TANAGRA

480 B.C. Themistocles becomes leader of Athens, Xerxes defeats Greek army under Leonidas at Thermopylae. Athenians flee to Salamis. The Persian fleet is defeated at the Battle of Salamis.

479 B.C. Persians retreat after losing Battle of Plataea to Spartans.

461 B.C. Pericles becomes leader of Athens and the Golden Age of Athens begins.

431 B.C. Beginning of Peloponnesian Wars. Thebans attack Plataea, Athens' ally. Attica invaded.

430 B.C. Plague in Athens. Athenians depose Pericles and then reappoint him. Attica invaded again.

429 B.C. Pericles dies. Siege of Plataea.

428 B.C. Cleon, leader of pro-war group, opposes Nicias.

425 B.C. Thucydides begins to write history of the war.

422 B.C. Cleon killed in Thrace.

421 B.C. Peace of Nicias signed by Athens and Sparta.

415 B.C. Alcibiades, Lamachus, and Nicias command expedition to Sicily. Alcibiades recalled, flees to Sparta.

413 B.C. Athenian forces in Sicily wiped out.

411 B.C. Sparta and Persia sign treaty.

405 B.C. Sparta defeats Athenian fleet at Aegospotami.

401 B.C. 10,000 Greeks join Cyrus of Persia's army. After death of Cyrus, the Athenian Xenophon leads the Greeks home.

399 B.C. Death of Socrates.

347 B.C. Death of Plato.

343 B.C. Aristotle tutors the young Alexander, son of King Philip of Macedonia.

338 B.C. Philip invades Greece and wins Battle of Chaeronea.

336 B.C. Philip is assassinated and is succeeded by Alexander, who is elected general of the Greeks.

333 B.C. At battle of Issus, Alexander defeats Darius of Persia.

331 B.C. Alexander conquers Egypt and defeats Persian army at Gaugamela.

330 B.C. Darius dies. Alexander subdues Iran.

323 B.C. After Alexander's death, his empire is divided into three parts. Antigonus claims Greece.